Caleb

"Take ... t caused the tip of the knife to slice against Lydia's jawline. She cried out in pain and closed her eyes as warm drops of blood trickled onto her shoulder.

Caleb halted. "Okay, okay. I'm staying put. Just put down the knife."

"Yeah," Kid laughed, his voice a trifle high. "Yeah. Maybe I will get rid of this thing."

Lydia dared to open her eyes and saw the knife waving perilously close to her face. She felt Cooley fumbling with something else behind her. Suddenly she knew.

"Caleb!" she shouted.

In an instant, Kid Cooley shoved her aside, sending her sprawling against the house.

She tried to gain some sort of foothold, anything, but it was all in vain. Everything seemed to be happening in slow motion.

Deafening shots echoed around her. As she crumpled to the ground, she felt her head hit something. Piercing pain rammed through her skull. Darkness swallowed her up.

GLORIA BRANDT makes her home in Wisconsin with her husband and four young daughters. Gloria says "I always want to encourage people that no matter what their circumstances or background, there is hope." *The Mountain's Son* is her first historical novel.

Other books by Gloria Brandt

HEARTSONG PRESENTS
HP174—Behind the Scenes

The Mountain's Son

Gloria Brandt

Heartsong Presents

To my big brother, Tim, who placed my first Louis L'Amour book in my hands. Love you, buddy!

And to the twins. . .we'll see you on the other side.

Special thanks, as always, to Sally. "Four score and seven years ago. . ." No kidding! Thanks for being my prodder, my eagle eyes, and my cheering section.

A note from the author:

I love to hear from my readers! You may correspond with me by writing:

Gloria Brandt
Author Relations
PO Box 719
Uhrichsville, OH 44683

ISBN 1-57748-322-7

THE MOUNTAIN'S SON

Cover illustration by Chris Cocozza.

PRINTED IN THE U.S.A.

one

May 1880

Silent streams of dusty sunlight radiated through the thick glass window, warming the already stifling air in the crowded train car chugging steadily down the endless rails.

Lydia Bennet sighed as she once again adjusted her position in the worn cloth seat. Momentarily tearing her gaze away from the soot-streaked pane, she caught her father's eye directly across from her, and he winked, an infectious smile spreading across his boyish face, making him appear a decade younger than his forty-five years. As usual, she found herself grinning back.

"Lydia, would you stop your fidgeting?" her mother scolded in hushed tones. "You're going to wrinkle your dress worse than it is already. Honestly, by your nonstop wriggling about, one would guess you to be a mere ten-year-old imp." She pressed her thin lips into a tight line as her steely blue gaze pierced Lydia's light green eyes.

"Yes, Mother." Lydia tried not to roll her eyes as she turned back toward the view outside, the only outlet for her varied feelings.

Several seconds of welcomed silence passed before her mother started in again. "I still don't know why you didn't book us a private cabin, John. Riding with these hordes of people has just about done me in." Leaning closer to him, she added with a whisper, "And by the stench of things, I believe some of them don't ever bathe." She pressed a lacy perfumed handkerchief to her nose.

Lydia felt her teeth starting to grind as she began the almost habitual process of taking slow calming breaths. How on earth did Father put up with her?

"Now, Mary," he began in his low, patient voice. "You know we needed to spare as much money as we could for this trip to the Wyoming Territory. Starting up a mercantile takes a good amount of capital—it means doing without frills for a while."

Mother let out a huff. "I still don't see why you found it necessary to up and leave our already thriving store in Independence."

"It was time for a change." He picked up the newspaper spread across his lap and snapped it into place. Lydia knew he considered the conversation to have ended.

Her mother turned toward Lydia's older sister, Sophia, whose frail frame had barely changed position in the last several hours. "Just wait until you see the patterns that are coming with our bolts of material. Some of them are simply wonderful!"

A wan smile appeared on Sophia's heart-shaped face.

Lydia gave a half smirk as she discreetly shook her head. Fashions. . .what a bore! She'd be only too glad to get to the small territorial town, where they'd be making their new home. Perhaps now that they'd actually left teeming Independence, her mother would ease up on her strict rules of dress. Even now Lydia muttered under her breath at the horrid confinement of the whalebone stays in her corset. Definitely not a comfort measure when traveling on a less-than-smooth-riding passenger car.

The train's noisy chugging slowed as the clacking of the wheels gave way to piercing screeches of metal and hissing vapors of steam.

Lydia felt the flutterings of anticipation in her stomach. Were they finally here?

"All off for the town of Veteran!" the conductor bellowed.

She shared an excited smile with her father as the two eagerly jumped up from their seats, but her mother motioned them down with her delicate hand. "Sit, sit, you two. I refuse to be trampled by this mob. We will wait until we can disembark in an orderly fashion."

Lydia didn't try to mask her sigh of impatience.

Retrieving a small pocket mirror from her handbag, her mother smoothed her brown hair back toward its ever-present bun underneath her small plumed hat. She handed the mirror to Sophia. "You may use it when she's finished, Lydia."

Lydia turned back toward the view from her window, intently studying the crowds milling about on the wooden-planked platform. Her breathing began to quicken as she took in the wide variety of persons outside. Some were dressed similarly to her family; others wore more rugged clothes. Not the kind she'd seen in Independence on the members of the wagon trains, but a tougher, coarser attire like the cowboys and drovers her father had said filled much of this new area.

But even more spectacular were the mountains crowning the land off in the distance, their awesome peaks mingling with the wisps of clouds. Lydia refrained from pressing her nose against the dirty glass, but, oh, how she longed to really see those mountains. All the way from Missouri, she'd watched the flat prairie gradually give way to gently rolling hills with the promise of taller peaks on the horizon.

A gentle tap on her shoulder brought her back to reality. "Here, Lydia." Sophia meekly handed over the small looking glass, and Lydia smiled softly at her. She noticed her sister looked tired. Now that she thought about it, Sophia had looked worn out for quite some time. The dark circles underlining her pale blue eyes hadn't lessened any over their trip and had made her flawless skin appear a sickly white.

Positioning the tiny mirror before her, Lydia appeased her mother by checking her own appearance. She nearly laughed when she saw the reflection. Dozens of her red corkscrew curls were in massive disarray, defiantly slipping out of the elegant upsweep that her mother always insisted she wear. She even caught a twinkling flash in her light green eyes that belied their excitement over the new visions to behold.

Placing the mirror in her lap, she reached up to adjust the myriad of combs that held her thick hair in place.

A shout rang out from the railroad platform.

Lydia whipped around in her seat just in time to see two men arguing. They seemed quite near coming to blows as a small crowd gathered around them.

Primping long forgotten, Lydia sprang up. Before her mother or anyone else could stop her, she squeezed her skirt's layers of blue ruffles past her mother's and Sophia's knees and bolted for the rear door.

"John, stop her!" registered momentarily as Lydia bounded down the steps in what she knew was a most unladylike manner. Her pace quickened as she heard the heavier clomps of her father's boots following her to the outer edge of the growing circle.

"I'll be takin' yer guns, fellas," a man shouted, stepping into the melee. "If yer gonna be a fightin', you'll be doin' it fair and square."

An arm brushed against Lydia's and she turned to see her father standing next to her, peering above the crowd for a better view. They threw one another a conspiratorial grin.

"John Avery Bennet!" The pitch turned more than one head. "I declare! What are you trying to subject our daughter to? I insist you tear yourself away from this mob of thrill-seekers at once. At once, I say!"

A few muffled titters came from the group. Her mother narrowed her icy blue eyes. "John. Lydia. Come along." Her tone left no question as to the seriousness of her anger, so the two rebel Bennets rejoined her.

After seeing to their trunks and making sure that all the supplies they'd needed were accounted for, the family walked toward the local hotel.

Lydia tried not to peer too obviously in the direction of the saloons as they passed by on the opposite side of the dirt street. Jolly, careless tunes tumbled out into the late afternoon air from several of the batwing doors. Occasionally she'd catch a glimpse of a heavily made-up woman prancing around the bar in lace and ruffles of black and red.

"Disgraceful hussies," Mother hissed, shaking her head.

"Now don't go jumping to too many conclusions about this

place," Lydia's father broke in. "It seems to me that Independence had its share of saloon girls as well."

Mother hiked her chin and looked painfully indignant while Lydia pursed her lips together to keep from laughing.

Once they'd acquired rooms at the two-story clapboard hotel, Sophia and her mother retired to the rooms to freshen up and rest.

Lydia's father turned to her and asked, "Would you care to join me on the jaunt to the livery? I need to inquire about a wagon and horses to get our start up to Darby."

"Oh, yes!" Lydia hastily fell in step beside her father down the wooden sidewalk.

Neither spoke as they took in their surroundings. Veteran wasn't a huge town, but it was large enough.

Lydia broke the silence. "Darby isn't this large, is it?"

"No, it's a good deal smaller. But it will do for us. And it sounds like the folks there will be grateful to have a general store once again. They've been having to make some mighty long trips to neighboring towns."

Lydia picked up her skirts as they stepped down from the wooden walk onto the dusty street. "I can't wait to see it. It will be such a welcome change from Independence."

For quite some time Lydia had felt a restlessness—one she couldn't really identify. After her father had announced their pending move, she'd guessed the change might be the thing to cure her growing uneasiness.

They continued in silence, Lydia trying to think of what life on a wagon train would be like. She knew the trip to Darby would take several days, but all she cared was that she would finally be able to be outside, living and breathing that wonderful air, taking in the rugged mountain majesty.

Without warning, her father grasped her arm and pulled her back. A wagon thundered in front of them. Lydia's breath caught in her throat as she clutched the bodice of her dress.

"Have to keep your head out of the clouds, Lydia." Her father's light green eyes twinkled as he let her go.

Even while the warmth stole across her cheeks, she knew

he understood. They were much alike.

Smells of leather, manure, and horse wafted into the street long before they stepped into the stables. While her father went in search of the livery hand, Lydia took the opportunity to stroll down the middle alley, admiring the beautiful animals in the stalls.

A large shiny roan caught her eye, and she stepped around the front of the enclosure to have a better look at him. The animal's round brown eyes glanced at her, and he nickered gently as he tossed his nose in her direction.

"Oh, you beautiful thing," Lydia crooned. She cautiously reached out a hand, and the animal shied away. "Don't worry, I won't hurt you." The gelding swung his head back toward her. "That's right." She again eased her fingers outward, ever so gently stroking the velvety soft skin on his nose. His warm breath came out in little puffs as he nuzzled into her touch.

"Uh, miss," a voice startled her and she tore her hand away, making the horse shy again.

"Yes."

A young sandy-haired man she figured to be close to her own age stepped around the side of the stall, his wide gray eyes clouded with concern. "It'd be best iffin' you leave that horse be."

"Oh. I'm quite sorry. I didn't realize. . .I was just admiring him."

"No harm done, I 'magine. Bit surprised he took to ya, though. Ain't much of a people horse."

"Hm. He seems so friendly." Lydia resisted the urge to give the reddish coat another pat and stepped out to follow the young man back into the alley.

"He's a new boy, that 'un. Ain't been broke yet."

"I see. Someone owns him?" she asked as she sidestepped to avoid some fresh evidence of a horse.

"Jonas owns him. . .like all the good ones that come through here."

"Who's Jonas?" Lydia looked up and saw her father talking with the livery manager some yards away. It took her several seconds to realize that the hand hadn't answered her. She glanced over to find him staring at her incredulously.

"You new here?"

"Yes. My parents are starting up the mercantile in Darby. That's my father up ahead."

He nodded in confirmation. "Well, that'd explain it."

"Explain what?"

"That you don't know Jonas."

Lydia merely nodded her head and considered the subject closed. So, she didn't know this Jonas man. She imagined she'd learn about everyone in good time.

Finally reaching her father, she stopped and waited close by until he'd finished his business with the manager.

"Ready, Lydia?" He joined her and offered his arm as they stepped back outside into the bright sunlight. There before the door sat a wide, flat wagon and a team of strong-looking horses.

After assisting Lydia up to the buckboard, her father climbed aboard himself and gathered up the slack reins. Instead of motioning for the horses to pull ahead, he grinned at Lydia mischievously as he studied her intently.

"What?" she asked.

"Would you care to drive to the station?"

Lydia barely caught the squeal of delight before it escaped from her lips. After all, her mother was right. She wasn't a young girl anymore. She had celebrated her eighteenth birthday last month. Perhaps it was time to grow up. . .a little bit.

She smiled broadly at her father as she grasped the reins from his hands. "Okay, boys, let's go." With a quick snap of the leather, the team took off with a jolt. Despite her best intentions, Lydia was unable to restrain her laughter as the team trotted down the main street.

❧

With a blurring flash and a loud whir, the hemp rope stung the air as Caleb tossed the lasso toward the yearling's rear feet. Quickly wrapping the slack over the pommel of the saddle, he skidded his agile horse to a stop and waited until the red and white Hereford fell to the ground with a grunt. Almost immediately, wiry Jake Turley, the ranch foreman, stepped in, grabbing the forelegs and head while Willy Albert, the bunkhouse cook and jack-of-all-trades, placed the red-hot iron across the rear flank, where they met with a sizzle and a thin trail of smoke. Several other hands stepped in to cut the identifying notch in the ear, and then the "medicine men" with their pots of disinfectant smeared the wounds.

As quickly as the process had begun, it was done. The animal scrambled to his feet, eager to rejoin the rest of the herd.

"That's the last of 'em," Willy called out as he replaced the branding iron near the fire, then straightened his burly form.

"Good." Caleb wound the rope quickly into a neat coil, adjusted his black Stetson, and headed his horse through the ambling stock, taking a quick inventory one last time. The hint of a smile crossed his lean face as he studied the rugged steers. An innate sense of pride always passed through him when he saw the box brand with the tail of the C forming the top of the J. The numbers were building again despite the harsh winter last year—no thanks to the bank. He'd done it all with sheer determination and stubbornness, refusing to quit. And it had finally paid off.

"What d'ya say?" Willy sauntered up from behind, removing a faded gray derby that had seen better days.

"A good bunch."

Willy nodded. "Sight better than last year's anyhow."

Caleb let out a small laugh, remembering the pathetic herd of the year before. They had never quite gotten over that harrowing winter. There were few to sell for profit, and most ended up being the contents of Willy's stew.

"Pity there'll be no long drive this time."

Removing his hat, Caleb brushed the sweat from his brow with the back of his sleeve. He nodded. The three-day drive to Veteran was still necessary, but he knew that Willy would miss the months on the trail as much as he did.

"Ah, well," the old hand continued. "Gives us more time to

be seein' to things 'round here, eh? One o' the blessin's of the railroad, I guess."

Firmly replacing the dusty Stetson, Caleb shot the gray-haired, wise-eyed man a look. "I imagine you'll be tryin' to get me paired off now, hm?"

Willy's eyes widened. "Me? Nope. From where I stand it seems you don't need much help in that area. Quite a sight goin' to town—watchin' them young fillies in skirts and ribbons flock 'round ya so." He shook his head. " 'Sides, I figger iffin' you'd a mind to, you'd a been married long afore now. Ain't many fellas 'round that ain't married when they're nigh on thirty years old."

A half smirk played with Caleb's lips as he tugged on the reins to turn his horse around. "Now you're sayin' I'm old?" he asked as he began to trot off.

"Not at that," Willy called after him. "Just sayin' that youth is wasted on the young."

Caleb chuckled as he headed toward the stables. Reaching the door, he swung down from the saddle and lit a lantern to brighten the dimming light of dusk.

From the opposite end of the horse barn, quick footsteps tapped toward him. He continued uncinching the saddle. "Hi, Jimmy," he said as he hung his tack on the proper hook.

"Hi." Jimmy Tucker's voice still held the same breath of excitement that it had when he'd first come to visit the ranch. His older brother, Hal, was one of the many hired hands, and Jimmy often tagged along, eager to learn the life of a cowboy. At eleven he was slightly overeager, but he showed promise in sticking to a task. He seemed genuinely grateful that Caleb took the time to teach him and now seemed to be trying in earnest to be everything that Caleb was.

Caleb turned toward the freckle-faced boy. "Were you running?"

A flame of color rushed up the lad's face, nearly matching the shade of his ruffled hair. Jimmy nodded glumly.

"No need spookin' the horses by runnin' through the barn, right?"

Another nod as he kicked at the scattered bits of hay on the floor.

Caleb gave him a sympathetic smile, remembering how it felt to be young and eager. "So, what is it?"

The bright blue eyes flashed up again, relieved at being forgiven. "Yer new gelding. It's here. Frank just came back from town and said it was delivered to the stables from the train just yesterday."

"Well, now. That is good news, isn't it?" He clapped the young man on the back. "Thanks, Jimmy."

The boy nodded excitedly and turned to leave almost on a run but then caught himself and walked briskly toward the opposite door. Halfway there, he turned back around. "Think I might come with you when you bring him home?"

Caleb finished leading his horse into his stall and leaned back into the alleyway. "Sorry, Jimmy. I need to get some extra supplies this trip. Maybe next time."

The sigh of disappointment was muted by a small grin covering the lad's sunburned cheeks. "Really? Next time?"

Caleb nodded as he fastened the gate behind him.

"Thanks, Mr. Jonas. Thanks a lot!"

two

Lydia stuffed the last of her gowns into the trunk and sighed as she snapped it closed. Raised voices carried through the adjoining door as her parents haggled over the latest disagreement. Those arguments always seemed to naggle at the pit of her stomach, and this one was no exception. It was probably even worse, since she knew very well that she was the cause . . .again.

She let her gaze drift from the door to the window, where Sophia sat in quiet repose, seemingly studying the street. "Sophia?"

"Hm?" came the mild reply.

Lydia joined her sister on the edge of the bed, gazing at the small bustle of people and horses making their way down the main street. "How are you doing?"

Sophia's pale blue eyes found Lydia's. "What do you mean?"

"Well, you've been looking tired lately. I just wanted to make sure you're all right."

A thin, frail hand moved to rest over Lydia's. "I'm okay, Lydia. Thank you for being concerned."

Lydia knew there was something more, and now might be the last time to discuss it before they left for the journey to their new home. "Sophia. Listen to me. I know that there's something—"

The separating door suddenly burst open and both of the girls found themselves looking into the tear-filled eyes of their mother.

"I honestly hope you're satisfied," she hissed, her gaze boring holes into Lydia. "It's not enough that I've tried to raise you two to be proper young ladies, but. . .but then you have a father who refuses to. . ." She sputtered into a flustered huff and stormed through the door into the hallway.

Their father came in several seconds later in a somewhat calmer state. He mutely stood with his hands in the pockets of his trousers, looking at the floor. When he raised his head to face them, an unmistakable sadness filled his eyes. "Sophia," he said softly. "I believe your mother's ready to leave for the stage station."

Sophia quickly got up from her place on the bed and grabbed her reticule and several other items before pausing at the door's threshold. Lydia knew what her sister was waiting for. . .what she, herself, was waiting for.

Her father's eyes finally met hers and she unconsciously held her breath as she waited for him to speak. The corners of his mouth just barely twitched.

"You heard me, Sophia." His gaze never left Lydia's face. "Your mother's waiting. Your sister and I will meet up with you in Darby."

Lydia watched as Sophia crossed the floor and placed a kiss on their father's freshly shaven cheek. Just before exiting, she turned and gave Lydia a cheerful wink.

In a flash, Lydia was on her feet and scurrying over to envelop her father in a warm embrace. "Oh, thank you, Daddy."

"Now," he half-heartedly complained as he pried her arms from him. "Don't go on so about it. But. . ." He pointed a finger in her direction. "I'm glad you are thankful. It took a small war to win that one. The mere idea of having one of Mary Bennet's daughters taking part in a makeshift wagon train more than just ruffled her feathers." He squared his shoulders, readjusting his shirt sleeves as if shirking off the whole episode.

Lydia nodded in the most serious face she could muster and quickly turned around. She glanced down at the traveling suit her mother had chosen for her that morning, not taking too much time to study its intricacies. As she headed for the valise that held the looser fitting "sacks," as her mother deemed them, she couldn't resist smiling at the thought of her corset in a discarded, jumbled heap.

❧

After several hours in the rising sun, bouncing and jostling over the rough terrain, Lydia began to wonder if she'd made a mistake in wanting to come along on the more than forty-mile journey. But a brief thought of being enclosed in a stuffy stage with her mother, sister, and very possibly other companions made her immediately grateful once again for her choice.

She shifted her position on the hard seat, padded only with a thin blanket. Her father must have seen her motion, one of many in the last half hour. "Yeah. I know. My tail's gettin' a little on the raw end, too." Lydia burst into laughter at the same time the train master called for a halt.

Needing no further coaxing, she jumped to the ground almost before the wheels had stopped rolling. She looked ahead to the seven other wagons. It was a small train compared to the sea of Conestogas that used to flood the outer areas of Independence. But these days, her father had said, most of the westward trains were things of the past. Of the few that were with them now, several also had Darby as their destination. *At least I'll get to know some of our neighbors right away,* Lydia thought.

She made her rounds of the wagon, making sure the waterproofed canvas was remaining secure at all the grommets, while her father checked the harnesses on the team of horses.

It seemed they'd hardly finished their lunch of dried beef sandwiches and several of the juicy apples they'd purchased when Mr. Wainright, the train master, hollered the go-ahead. Lydia stood up and brushed the dust from her brown calico prairie dress.

"Why don't you try walking for a while?" her father asked as he climbed back up into his driver's position. "I've seen some of the others doing that up ahead. Might be a nice break."

"All right." Lydia stood off to the side as the wagons started their slow roll forward and fell into step a short distance away to keep out of the dust. Fortunately the small herd of cattle that a traveling farmer was guiding to his newly purchased land was traveling on the other side of the train. At least she didn't have to deal with the swirling dust kicked up from their hooves. . .or the scattered droppings.

"Hello, Miss Bennet," a raised voice came from behind her.

Lydia winced. There were other pests to deal with. Hoping the interloper would leave if she pretended not to hear him, she quickened her determined pace.

"Ma'am?"

No such luck. He drew his horse right alongside of her, slowing to match her strides.

"Good day, Mr. Cooley." No sense in being rude.

"Right nice day, isn't it?" He spat a squirt of tobacco juice into the dust ahead in a sort of punctuation.

"Yes, indeed." She turned her head toward the outrider and saw his boyish face streaked with dirt, an irritating grin spread across his cheeks. As innocent as he looked, Lydia didn't trust him. He'd dogged her path since learning she'd be on the train, and there was something in his steely gray eyes and cocky bearing she didn't trust.

Returning her gaze to the wagons ahead of her, she offered him an exit. "Won't Mr. Reese be needing help with his cattle? That is what he hired you for, isn't it?"

"Aw, Doug and Bill can manage fine for a minute. Just wanted to make sure our little flower was sittin' pretty back here."

Lydia swallowed the urge to gag. She managed a polite smile. "I'm fine, thank you. But perhaps you'd better get back to your post. We wouldn't want anything to happen to those cows."

He threw his head back in a mocking laugh. "Nothin', I mean nothin', will happen while I'm herdin' 'em." He patted the holster resting on his leg.

"Yes. I'm sure."

"Cooley!" a shout came from farther up the line.

"What!"

"Get up here! I'm not payin' ya to spend yer time lollygaggin' around." Mr. Reese waved his arm at the herd before trotting his horse back to the opposite side of the wagons.

Lydia watched Kid Cooley mutter something under his breath as a scowl darkened his ruddy face. But as quickly as it had appeared, it vanished again, leaving a somewhat leering smile. "Guess I'm needed up there. Maybe I'll see you after we stop for the night."

Lydia didn't even nod, much less answer. The less encouragement she gave him, the better.

She expelled a heavy sigh of relief as he finally galloped back to his cronies. Hearing their raucous laughter, she didn't have to guess what they'd be discussing. But at least she was alone now.

She let her eyes wander over the distant peaks of the Laramie Mountains. They were so beautiful. She longed to see them up close. . .to ride through them and experience them first hand. Would she ever be able to? Darby was a good distance away from that range. Probably a good thirty miles. Still, if she could ever get a horse, maybe. . .

❧

Caleb pushed his dun through the growing dusk of afternoon. The saddle creaked as he shifted position to study the fuzzy green patches of grass that kept showing more and more of themselves as May pressed on. Pastureland would be good this year.

When the sun finally slipped beneath the curve of a distant hill, he drew his horse into a small hollow near Chugwater Creek. The natural walls provided an enclosure, and he knew any fire he built would be mighty hard to spot. Even so, he would sleep away from the flames, near the crest. His vantage point would be much broader. Besides, he knew that Indians would think a white man's position would be near the warmth of a fire.

He hadn't had any unfriendly encounters with the Sioux for years, but caution based on experience always took over—especially when he was out in the open like this.

Picketing his horse in a grassy patch near the creek, he laid his faded black hat aside and built a small fire, then fried up the bacon and beans that Willy had been generous enough to pack for him. He glanced around in the creeping darkness. The usual night sounds—the snapping and crackling of the twigs in the fire, the dusting of breeze that intermittently played with the cottonwood leaves, and the creek's quiet gurgling as it flowed past—always comforted him somehow.

It had been a long while since he'd been away from the ranch. Roundup took a goodly amount of time, and he now realized how much he'd missed these excursions. He felt at home.

Draining the last of his coffee, Caleb walked down to the creek's shallow edge and rinsed his dishes, then bathed his face and neck in the coolness of the clean water. Glancing up at the star-speckled sky, he noticed the nearly full moon. It cast an odd glow on the rolling landscape, turning everything an ethereal color.

He was about to turn back toward his horse to retrieve his bedroll when he heard a sound. He stood stock-still and listened. At first he heard nothing, but a minute or so later he heard the noise again. This time he recognized it as voices.

Moving quietly toward his horse, he pulled his Winchester from the boot near the saddle and crouched down as he stepped up toward the top of the small knoll. A smile of relief came across his face. He let the barrel rest beside him. In an open area, not too much farther upstream from him, a small group of covered wagons formed a circle around the large campfire in the middle. This must be the train coming up to Darby. He went back to his horse and returned with his field glasses. Peering through them intently, he searched for any familiar faces around the fire's light.

Old Sam Wainright was there, as usual with any train heading this way. Most of the others looked new: some young families with small children nodding off in their parents' laps, a few young bucks who were probably along to help with the small herd of cattle he'd seen grazing not far away.

He was about to lay down his glasses when a flash near the creek caught his eye. Readjusting them, he squinted until he could make out a form walking briskly away from the circle toward the water's edge. He waited a moment until the person stepped into a patch of moonlight where no trees cast dark shadows over the ground.

It was a girl. No, a woman. Inching up the incline on his elbows, he watched with renewed interest. The distance combined with the darkness made it hard to see her face, but he couldn't miss her hair. A tumble of bright red curls fell freely down her shoulders in sharp contrast with the moonlit white of her nightdress.

What was she doing out there away from everyone else? Now that curiosity had the best of him, he continued to watch her. She sat down near the bank, her arms propped on her raised knees for some time. How long she stayed that way he wasn't sure. Occasionally she'd lift her coppery head and look up at the sky, as if she were searching for something.

Finally she stood. She strode over to a nearby tree, plucking several leaves from its branches. He continued to watch, fascinated. When she'd retraced her steps toward the water, she stooped down and placed something in the gently flowing current. He tried to focus in on it. It looked almost like a. . . well, a small boat. Complete with a tiny white sail. He trained the glasses back on her as she watched it slowly drift away.

Another movement caught his eye in a grouping of trees behind her. He squinted in concentration. Although he couldn't pick out anything unusual, a feeling of distrust shot through him. One that he'd learned to rely on long ago. Momentarily putting down the field glasses, he lifted his chin in the air and let out the sad cry of a wolf. He'd heard it and practiced it enough that he knew it would fool most.

Grabbing up the lenses, he found her again. She'd turned around from her position and, clutching her arms about her chest, was standing quite still. She'd heard it. It had the effect he'd hoped for. She began sprinting back toward the wagons, her white gown billowing out behind her.

Then he waited. A considerable amount of time elapsed before his patience paid off. Slowly, stealthily, another figure emerged from the trees. A man stood there a moment, seeming to look in Caleb's direction before he began a brisk walk toward the circle as well.

Feeling that all was well, Caleb finally unrolled his blankets and stretched out his long legs beneath the vast expanse of sky. He frowned as he thought back over the episode. He began to wonder if perhaps the man in the trees might have been the lady's husband just trying to surprise her. But almost as soon as he thought of it, he discarded the notion. There was something menacing about the whole situation—the way that man had been hiding behind those trees. No, Caleb was confident that he'd done the right thing. Now it was no longer his concern.

Rolling over, he pulled his Winchester closer to him and closed his eyes. Far off, a wolf cried out and another answered its lonely call.

three

Caleb's eyes opened almost involuntarily, fixing themselves on the still-darkened sky. He scanned quickly for the Big Dipper, checking its location in relation to the bright North Star. Time to get moving. It would be sunrise in a couple hours. He tossed aside his blanket and quickly rolled and tied everything up.

He started down the short incline toward the glowing embers of his fire. Almost as an afterthought he looked over his shoulder at the group of wagons. Not much sign of life, although he knew they would be up and running within the next hour.

After coaxing the dying fire with fresh fuel, he headed to the creek to fill his small coffee pot. As he dipped the container into the clear water, he lifted his head to study the surrounding area in the vague light of predawn. Glancing once again at the heavens, he saw the stars' bright points fading as fingers of grayish light began to streak across the sky. He took a deep breath of contentment, filling his lungs with the invigorating air. Then he noticed it. A small patch of white floating against the creek's dark depths. A good-sized dead limb was protruding into the water from the shoreline, and near its tip rested a small vessel with a tiny sail.

Caleb had nearly forgotten the previous night's incident, but now he frowned in curiosity. Leaving his water-filled pot on the ground, he stepped toward the limb and broke off a smaller branch. Squatting precariously near the water's edge, he reached out with the stick until he snagged the tiny boat and pulled it ashore.

The sail was a heavy piece of paper, pierced on each end. He slipped it off the mast and found it was folded in half and appeared to have writing on it. While carefully opening the paper, he wondered about how strange this was. He'd heard of people so lonely they'd tied notes to tumbleweeds and watched them bounce off into the distance. He supposed this was no different. Yet he began to wonder if he ought to be reading it at all. No two ways about it—the message had to have been written by the woman he'd seen last night. Maybe it was personal. Then again, she had just let it go. . . .

He lowered his eyes to the tiny missive, squinting at the neat, feminine cursive. After the first two lines he frowned and surveyed the rest of the page. This was more like a. . . poem. Sighing, he started over again.

Could one e'er be content
with a dream subdued
A tune sprung forth
yet no melody ensued

If a quiet green glen
refused its face
would not a sun set
amidst tears of disgrace

I know a tree
its leaves would dry
if no wind caressed it
in song passing by

Should a heart be no different
a soul less than these
to thirst for fulfillment
like a song. . .the sun. . .the trees.

He read it again. And again. Typical. Another unhappy wife dragged west against her wishes. It reinforced what he'd known from the start. Not many women belonged in the back of beyond—and he certainly wouldn't be foolish enough to try and ask a wife to endure what made most men turn and head home with their tails between their legs.

Shaking his head, he stuffed the paper into his shirt pocket as he continued on with his task of making his morning coffee.

❧

After she'd splashed the night-chilled water over her face and neck, Lydia pulled on her prairie dress and began working at the tangled mass of knots in her curls. Goodness, what she wouldn't give for normal, straight hair.

With a sigh, she lifted the flap and stepped from the back of the wagon. The smells of nearby breakfast fires greeted her, urging her to get on with gathering a few pieces of wood as well. Her father would be finished caring for the horses soon and would want coffee.

She blew a loose strand of red hair away from her face and gave up on the idea of pinning her hair up today. Dropping the comb back into her small valise, she satisfied herself by merely fastening it securely at the back of her neck. At least it would be out of the way.

Glancing around, she noticed that nearly everyone had their fires going. She chastised herself for her slowness and scanned the area for some signs of fallen wood. Where had she seen some? A healthy shiver ran up her spine as she slowly turned and faced the small grove of cottonwoods she'd visited the night before. There had been numerous sticks and loose branches there.

Lydia released a shuddering breath as she studied the surrounding lay of the land, in particular the small knoll south of the creek. Did wolves come out in the daytime as well?

A hand gripped her shoulder.

She whirled around, nearly losing her balance.

"Lydia?"

"Oh," she gasped, trying not to laugh at her own jumpiness. "Good morning, Daddy."

"Are you all right?" He narrowed his eyes to study her.

"Yes, fine." She smiled wobbly.

He nodded, as if to reassure himself, before replacing his bowler on his graying black hair. "Breakfast is ready, if you're hungry." He started toward the front of the wagon.

"It is?" She traipsed behind him, feeling rather foolish.

"I figured I'd let you sleep in this morning. You seemed pretty tuckered out last night, missing the singing at the fire and all. And I noticed you didn't sleep too well."

She took a seat on a log placed next to the fire. "Sorry if my tossing and turning disturbed you." She eagerly accepted the bowl of steaming oatmeal, habitually blowing on the first spoonful. "Daddy?"

"Hm?" He looked up from his own breakfast.

"Do, um. . .do wolves come out. . .during the day?"

"Wolves? Not generally, I don't think. They seem to like the cover of the dark."

She nodded in relief.

"But then," he added in a low voice, "there are those who dare the daylight." She glanced up in alarm to see him with a serious frown across his brow. His gaze seemed to be directed behind her. "Mornin'," he stated.

Lydia turned to find a smiling Kid Cooley had approached.

"Good morning, Mr. Bennet. Miss Bennet."

"Good morning, Mr. Cooley." She turned back toward the fire.

"You know," Kid started, "Sam says that we're makin' real good time on this trip. Figures we'll be in Darby by late tomorrow afternoon."

"So, I'd heard," Lydia's father replied.

"Well, I don't know if ya knew, but there's usually a social and a dance at the schoolhouse on Saturday night. I was wondering if maybe Miss Bennet would come with me."

Lydia, with her back still to Kid Cooley, looked at her father with wide eyes. He made no comment, but calmly began taking a spoonful from his bowl again. Wasn't he going to say anything?

"Miss Bennet?" The sound of shuffling feet accompanied the address.

"Well, Mr. Cooley. . ." It suddenly dawned on her. She was eighteen now. She answered for herself. She took a fortifying breath and turned to face him again. "I thank you for the offer, but I'm afraid my first several days in Darby will be spent helping my parents get the store established and our house in order."

He nodded curtly and replaced his dusty hat. "Another time then." He gave a brief smile before sauntering away.

Lydia watched her father with an amused expression. "Some dare the daylight, hm?" she whispered before she let loose a few quiet giggles.

Her father didn't seem to share her levity. "Be careful with that one, Lydia. I don't trust him."

"Oh, Daddy. I wouldn't go with him if he asked a million times. But I think he's fairly harmless."

He looked unconvinced but said nothing more. And Lydia, herself, remembered there was something about Kid Cooley that had sent warning signals off in her as well. Perhaps he would bear watching.

❧

The last rays of dusk were settling over the bustling town of Veteran as Caleb marched his gelding down the main thoroughfare. His stomach rumbled insistently when he passed the warmly lit windows of Mama Bailey's restaurant. The savory odor of roast and gravy quickly reminded him that his only meal that day had been a meager breakfast.

"To the stables first," he urged, and patted the thick, gray neck below him, knowing his horse was more than ready for his much earned rest and feed as well.

Passing by the building adjacent to the stables, Caleb raised a hand in greeting toward the blacksmith, who nodded before bending back over the upturned hoof of a horse.

His mount seemed to anticipate the arrival of fresh hay and grain, if his increased pace was any indication. Caleb reined in his eager traveling companion and swung down from the saddle.

A friendly voice came from the darkened doorway. "Evenin', Mr. Jonas."

"Howdy, Curtis."

"Been waitin' for ya."

Caleb led his horse into the dimly lit stables until he found an empty stall. "I imagine you have." He smiled over his shoulder at the young man. "You been takin' good care of him?"

"Yes, sir!"

"Good." He finished uncinching the saddle and lifted it off before urging the animal into the stall with a gentle slap on its flank. "So where is he?"

"This way."

Caleb hung his tack on the appropriate hook and followed. He paused when they approached the gelding, taking the time to study the contours of the animal's strong frame. Stepping to the side, he reached over the wooden plank partition and laid a gentle hand on the smooth chestnut-colored coat. He felt a skittish shiver.

Moving to the front, Caleb was met by two large brown eyes that seemed to assess him in the same manner. A half smile twitched at Caleb's mouth. "Hi there, buddy." The horse turned his head away for a second before bringing it back to study the strange man in front of him.

"Well, Curtis," Caleb said as he stepped back toward the stable hand. "Whaddya think?"

"Right nice. In fact, the best I can ever remember seein'."

Caleb nodded in agreement and cast back one last glance as they headed for the main door.

"He's brought lots of interest since he's been here anyway," Curtis offered.

Caleb cut a look his way. "What do you mean?"

The younger man's eyes widened as he caught the expression. "Oh, no. No buyers or nothin'. And we been keepin' a real close eye on him since he's come. But everybody seen him when he came down from the train. Not too many horses get shipped in, ya know. Much less from Texas."

Caleb inclined his head to one side in acknowledgment. As usual, gossip would be flying high. That was one thing he still hadn't been able to shake since coming back to the territory four years ago. People were sure up for a juicy bit of news about almost anybody, it seemed.

He halted his train of thought and realized he'd missed half of what young Curtis had just said.

"Told her not to touch him, but she didn't seem real afraid of what he might do. Course, I didn't figure she'd had much experience with unbroke horses. Not the way she was dressed anyway."

"What?"

Curtis turned to him. "The gal in the stable. She was in there talking to your new boy."

"What gal?"

He shrugged. "I dunno. Headed up to Darby. Reckon you'll see her there. Startin' up the mercantile again, I guess."

"Really." Caleb involuntarily quickened his step as they approached the steps of Mama Bailey's. "I imagine I will see her then. I'll tell you, it will sure be nice not having to trot all the way down here for supplies. It's been almost three years since the last owner left."

"Yeah, I guess so." Curtis stopped as they reached the front door. "Well, I'd better head back and make sure Ernie's all set up for his shift." He began the short jaunt back to the livery. "See ya at the Black Pearl later?"

"Aren't you a little young to be hangin' out in places like that?"

"Not as young as I used to be," he called back with a grin.

Caleb chuckled as he pushed open the front door. A noticeable hush fell across the room, and he tried to ignore the semidisguised stares. Finding a small table, he sunk into the chair and tried to hide behind the newspaper someone had left behind on the red-checkered tablecloth.

"Good evening, Mr. Jonas," a lilting voice said.

He peered across the top of the page and smiled when he saw the familiar face. "Hi, Moira."

"Hungry tonight?" Her bright blue eyes sparkled as she gave him a wide grin.

"Enough to eat a bear."

"Sorry. The closest we've got is beef." She smoothed back a wisp of blond hair from her face.

"Anything's fine, Moira. And some coffee, too, please. But only if you promise to dip your finger in it."

"My finger? Why?" Her light brows frowned in confusion.

"To sweeten it, of course." He was rewarded with a wide-eyed look as her cheeks took on a rosy glow. "Warm in the kitchen tonight, hm?" he teased.

Flustered, she wove her way to the kitchen door while he watched, amused.

He was about to turn his attention back to the paper when his keen hearing picked up a portion of a conversation on the other side of the room. Discreetly flipping the page, he managed a quick glance in that direction.

Two men were sitting at the corner table talking in hushed tones. One of them, judging by his vest, jeans, and boots, was a cowboy or hand. The other, facing away from Caleb, sported a finely cut suit that unquestioningly proclaimed its eastern origin. Caleb narrowed his eyes as he studied the dressier of the two, noting everything from his neatly groomed dark hair to his recently shined shoes.

A plate and silverware clattered in front of him, and he looked up at Moira's averted gaze. "Thanks. Looks mighty tempting." He smiled warmly at her as he laid aside his periodical.

"I'll bring your pie later," she answered shyly.

"Good enough."

As he delved into the hearty helping of roast, potatoes, and rich brown gravy, the conversation across the room grabbed his attention again. The cowboy seemed to be getting slightly worked up about something as the suited gentleman tried to calm him down.

Pieces of words and phrases drifted over occasionally, but Caleb didn't pay them much mind until he heard one word.

"A ranger!" the vested man said with an edge to his lowered voice.

Caleb tried not to bring up his eyes too quickly. The man in the suit shifted, as though suddenly uncomfortable, and slowly rose from the table. He dropped several coins near his empty plate while the other fellow sat there with a dejected look on his face.

The "suit" said something undecipherable before turning around. His long legs started him toward the door, but he paused when he met Caleb's stare. For a split second he looked almost startled. But if he had been, he recovered quickly and continued his exit.

A few minutes later, after Moira had brought Caleb's pie, the other man bolted up from the table and sauntered angrily across the floor. He didn't look at anyone or anything as he stomped out the door and into the early evening.

Caleb mused over the encounter for a moment and wondered why the well-dressed man would strike a chord of familiarity with him.

four

Lydia sighed in relief as she pushed the last bolt of fabric onto the lowest shelf and stepped back to survey her work. The rainbow of colored remnants filled a good portion of the store's south wall.

"Looks good, Lydia," her father commented from behind her.

Turning and smiling her appreciation, she headed over to help him finish stacking the earthenware dishes they would sell. Lydia found the clay's rough gray texture charming in its own way, although her mother had fairly steamed when she saw the crates of pottery.

"Where is the china. . .the-the crystal?"

"Mary," her father had sighed. "We're in a different place now. Darby isn't a booming town like Independence. People's needs here are different, not to mention their pocketbooks."

After the dismay and ensuing arguments over everything from the "overabundance of bullets and warring ammunition" to the "ridiculously short selection of fabrics," Lydia's mother had proclaimed herself tormented by a splitting headache and marched into their living quarters through a door in the rear of the store, demanding Sophia's help with some task or another.

Now the last rays of the early evening sun were beginning to fade as the glowing orange ball slipped behind the distant Laramie Peak.

Lydia crossed to the store's front window to watch the splendor of the colored sky.

"Beautiful place, isn't it?"

She glanced over at her father in half-surprise, not knowing when he'd approached. "It truly is. In a different, wild sort of way. I can't imagine why the previous owners would ever have wanted to leave. I'm so glad you brought us here."

Now it was his turn to smile at her. But a sadness in his eyes downplayed his grin. He placed his hands in his trouser pockets and released a breath. "Well, that's one of you anyway."

Lydia looked at his frowning profile. Poor Daddy. He deserved some happiness. If only Mother would support him more—support him, period.

With a cheerful voice, she said, "Oh, don't worry about Mother. She'll come around. Besides, I think Sophia's glad to be here. So that makes three of us—a proper democracy!"

His green eyes twinkled as he studied her. Suddenly the frown vanished and his handsome face lit up with a laugh. "All right, Miss Optimist. You've earned your rest. Why don't you get ready to retire for the night? Tomorrow's Sunday. We can finish up the rest of the sorting Monday."

"Thanks, Daddy."

Through the open doorway, from the white clapboard schoolhouse at end of the street, came the muted sounds of a fiddle and harmonica mingling with clapping, cheers, and the steady drum of boots against a hardwood floor.

Lydia leaned over and brushed a kiss across her father's stubbled cheek.

"Thinking of heading down that way?" He grinned as he nodded in the general direction of the dance.

"No," she answered. "I was thinking about heading out back and walking down to the river. Is that all right?"

"I guess so. Just be careful."

He'd barely given his permission before Lydia bolted through the front door and rounded the corner of the two-story building they were making their new business and home.

The sun had finally set and the waning light was beginning to be aided by the expansive moon. She hiked up her skirts and ran until she reached the river's edge, nearly breathless. This wide section of the North Platte River almost resembled a lake in its serenity, although the slightest current was still detectable in the moonlit waters.

Lydia plopped down onto the bank before she realized that

she'd probably pay for that move with several grass stains. Oh, well. Wasn't it worth it? Resting her elbows on her raised knees, she propped her chin on her hands and smiled. The view and the feeling that seemed to accompany it were too magnificent for words. Already she regretted when she'd have to leave for home, yet she was fortunate enough to have a small window right above her bed through which she could study this same scene.

She stayed for several more minutes before deciding she'd best start back. She still had to bathe tonight for church tomorrow. It would be good to be at services again. With their train trip and journey here, it seemed a good eternity since they'd been able to attend.

Picking herself up, she bid a farewell glance to the pastoral waters, silently thanking God for the incredible beauty of the place, and traipsed through the brushy grass that covered the distance between her and the store.

As she neared the rear entrance to their home, she distinctly heard her mother's voice. Its hushed yet forceful tones indicated there was something brewing. Definitely not ready to face that, she decided to take a quick stroll around the perimeters of the little town. She was hardly fit to be seen after toting dirty, dusty boxes most of the day, so she skirted around the backs of the establishments, taking note of the offshooting street of homes that ran parallel to the main street near the livery.

Lydia wasn't sure of the lateness of the hour, but the signs of life from the schoolhouse didn't show any indications of slowing down. With a quiet giggle she wondered if they'd be out before the morning church service.

Making a wide circle around the small building, she paused a distance from the windows and arched on tiptoes, trying in vain to see some of the action from a safe distance. That was all she needed—someone spotting her out here and wondering about her secretive spying.

She'd just ducked past the school's two privies when she heard voices. Her heart leaped into her throat as she scurried back to the cover of the tiny outbuildings. Sincerely hoping the closest one wasn't occupied, she flattened herself against the outside of the back wall and waited. So far, all she'd heard was a woman's voice, and she winced when she realized the lady and her companion were heading toward her hiding place.

"I thought you liked me."

A deep, throaty chuckle followed.

"Don't laugh at me! Honestly, you certainly know how to provoke a girl. Haven't you the least bit of interest in me at all?"

Lydia's eyes widened at the boldness of the young woman's statement.

" 'Course I do," the man replied.

Lydia took note of his odd voice. Low, yet soft. Almost like whispering, yet she could hear him.

"Hmmph!" the girl continued. "But I saw you dancing with Jenny Parker, and I know for a fact that she's chasing after Billy Johnson—"

"And Chad Stevens and Doc Foy and—" His raspy voice broke into a small laugh. "Priscilla, you should see the look on your face right now. Why, I believe. . .yep, I do believe it's a shade green."

The girl threw out her anger in a disgusted huff, and Lydia heard her rapidly swishing skirts moving away as she mumbled some nonsense about "We'll see who's jealous."

She didn't hear any more sounds and assumed the gentleman had followed his companion back to the ruckus of the school. She waited what she considered a safe amount of time and started toward the backs of the buildings on the opposite side of the main street.

The faint light of a lantern lit one window in the stables, and as Lydia watched, it extinguished. A strongly built fence formed a good-sized corral behind the building, and a few horses stood quietly grazing. She padded to the fence and, quickly glancing around, squeezed between the lowest and middle rails.

❧

Caleb unsuccessfully tried to hide an amused smile as anger flashed through Priscilla Davis's blue eyes. In keeping with his expectations, she stormed back toward the schoolhouse, her dark curls bouncing with each step.

Shaking his head, he moved up the small hill and sat down in the cover of a few trees. He imagined she'd stew about it for a while. Good enough, he thought. He'd had about his fill of socializing tonight anyway. He might as well head to his boarding house room for the night. Tomorrow's duties would call early, and he had much to accomplish before he started for home Monday morning.

It was when he started to stretch out his legs that he saw the person leaning against one of the outbuildings. Freezing in a half-standing position, he squinted against the darkness. In the shadows of the small shack, he couldn't tell much except that whoever it was was short.

He watched curiously as the figure peeked around the side of the building opposite where he was sitting. When she finally emerged from her hiding, Caleb started for a moment. The girl from the wagon train. He cocked his head in wonder as he watched her briskly run down to the area of the livery. Who on earth was this girl? She certainly seemed to enjoy stealing around at night, that was sure.

He left his spot on the hill and stealthily followed her to see what this mystery woman might do next. Catching up with her at the stables, he ducked behind the corner of the building just as she turned to look around. To his amazement, she climbed into the corral. Thinking of his unbroken horse, he nearly went in to fetch her out, but her calm movements made him hold back.

Somehow he wasn't surprised to see her approaching his horse. This must be the young lady that Curtis had been talking about, the one eyeing his new mount in the stables at Veteran. But why would she be interested in his horse?

He watched in fascination as she caressed the animal and spoke to him in low tones. Stepping forward slightly, he memorized the scene. He had to admit, it did make quite a picture. The girl with her blazing red hair standing near the similarly colored roan, both of them awash in the moon's muted light.

Captivated, he stole closer to the display, finding a convenient hiding place behind a series of large posts. Peering out, he found himself close enough to catch remnants of her conversation.

"Remember me, don't you?"

The gelding blew out several quick breaths through his nostrils before tossing his head in her direction.

"Sure you do." She ran a gentle hand across his cheek and neck. "You're a handsome boy. Is Darby going to be your new home, too?"

She remained quiet for a time, simply patting the unaccountably calm creature.

Far too soon for Caleb's liking, she moved away toward the fence. He stepped back into the darkness just before she lifted her eyes cautiously, hiked up the hem of her dress, and slid through the confining slats.

He continued to watch her while she rounded the far corner of the split-rail fence and again until she reached the confines of the nearby general store and disappeared inside.

Caleb lightly fingered the small slip of paper he'd kept in his shirt pocket. He'd have to pay a visit to that new store right soon.

❧

Lydia fidgeted against the stiffness of the wooden plank that served as the pew. For an early May Sunday it was unaccountably warm. She'd enjoyed her first church service, but she began to wish that the stout woman at the pump organ would hurry things along a bit on the last hymn. Even the poor organ seemed to heave its way through the notes, seemingly aware of the heat as well.

The last chord struck, Lydia managed to remain seated until Pastor Hodges made his way to the rear door. The small crowd around her rose simultaneously, everyone chatting and greeting one another in a friendly fashion.

"Lydia," her mother interrupted before she could bolt for the freshness of the outdoors. "There are several people I'd like you to meet."

Lydia sighed. Of course. They needed to establish a rapport with the townspeople, but, oh, it got dreadfully boring. She nodded and followed her mother to where her father and Sophia were already engaged in conversation with a dark-haired man in a suit. As Lydia approached, she noticed first the fellow's handsome blue eyes set off by his black curly hair. He seemed sincerely friendly as his easy smile peeked out from under a well-trimmed mustache.

"Lydia," her father paused in his conversation to take her elbow and usher her into the small circle. "This Dr. Jim Foy."

She gave him a polite smile. "Hello."

"Very nice to make your acquaintance, Miss Bennet." He tipped his head forward in an informal bow. "I was just telling your father how he'll have to keep a sharp eye out with two beautiful daughters new to the town." He and Mr. Bennet shared a chuckle at the exact same moment a small gathering of young men not so discreetly jerked their attention elsewhere.

Lydia felt her cheeks flame ever so slightly under the compliment and the scrutiny and looked to her sister for her reaction. Amazingly, Sophia's eyes, which were shining in a manner they hadn't in a long time, never left the young doctor's face. Lydia concealed a smirk and vowed to do some talking to her sister the moment they were alone.

"Lydia," her mother's voice rang in her ears. "Over here, dear." She beckoned her to another group of eager-looking faces. Lydia blew out a quiet breath and fastened on her best proper-daughter demeanor. Talking with Sophia would have to wait.

❧

Lydia splashed the last of the tepid water over her face and blotted it dry with a towel. Taking up her nearby candle, she moved down the narrow hall, tiptoeing past her parents' bedroom door and around the corner to the room she shared with Sophia.

Her sister was already in bed, a barely distinguishable form under the whiteness of the bedsheets. Lydia shuffled by the foot of Sophia's bed and around the shared chest of drawers that formed a sort of privacy wall between their two narrow cots.

Flopping down with relief, she extinguished the dying flame from the candle, leaned toward the small window near her headboard, and breathed in the night air. Once again she was grateful that this house had removable panes in the windows, especially in this heat.

The now waning moon tried earnestly to cast a glow on the sedate waters of the North Platte, but a few rogue clouds marred its attempts.

"Lydia?" Sophia's voice broke the stillness.

"Mm hmm?"

A moment of silence ensued, as if Sophia were carefully choosing her words. Lydia was used to that.

"Did you like him?"

Lydia smiled. So she didn't have to bring up this morning's subject after all. She decided to play innocent. "Who?"

A dense feather pillow came hurtling over the chest of drawers and landed just short of her bed.

A giggle escaped Lydia's lips as she swung out of bed, scooped up the errant pillow, and carried it over to its owner. Handing it to her sister, she took a seat on the edge of the thin mattress. "I suppose," she admitted. "He seemed nice enough." She tried to make out Sophia's features in the growing darkness. "I guess I don't have to ask if you did."

A sigh was the only response.

"Oh, Soph." Lydia grasped her sister's two dainty hands in her own. "I'm not sure what to think. That's the first time I've ever seen you so. . .so lit up."

A quiet laugh followed. Another oddity for her usually somber sister.

"Well," Lydia tried to sound pragmatic. "I hope it all works out for you. I just can't believe that—" She cut herself short before going on.

Sophia sat up. "Believe what?" she prompted.

"Well," Lydia hesitated, not sure how much she should say before it would be prodding. "I guess. . .I don't know. I guess I've never seen you like this before. I just thought it kind of odd, you know." She paused before going on. "I mean, here you are, twenty years old, and up until this time there's never been *anyone* who's made you give him a second glance."

Sophia was quiet. Then she laid back down against the softness of her pillow. "Maybe," she whispered.

Lydia was confused. Whatever she had said seemed to bring down that shroud of dark silence that had hung over her sister for nearly as long as she could remember. She definitely didn't want to be the one to cause that.

"Oh, here we are," Lydia piped up cheerily. "Two new maidens in a town full of eligible young men, and Independence is a long ways away." She reached down to give Sophia an impromptu hug. "And besides," she added over her shoulder as she made her way back to her own bunk. "I thought his eyes lingered over you considerably longer than is deemed necessary to polite conversation."

She half-expected another pillow toss toward her head but instead came Sophia's quiet voice. "Do you really think so?"

A swelling of compassion in Lydia's heart made her answer with all earnestness. "Yes, I really do."

That seemed to settle things. A brief moment later the only sound to be heard was the steady, contented breath of sleep from the other side of the room.

Lydia propped herself up on her elbows as she once again gazed out at the vast, rugged land outside her small window. The mountains were now only a dark mass in the shapeless night. "You've found your dream to follow, Soph. Now, for mine."

five

Monday morning dawned earlier than seemed civil, but the sheer excitement of the upcoming day drove Lydia from her bed. Tossing back her coverlet, she snuck past the still sleeping form of her sister. A contented look covered Sophia's face, the appearance of a long-needed and restful sleep.

Voices and puttering noises drifted up the narrow stairs from the family's living quarters. Dad and Mother were already up. Not surprising. Today was opening day at Bennet's Mercantile and Dry Goods, and lots of last-minute duties stared every one of them in the face.

But excitement prevailed in Lydia's attitude. She didn't stop to think twice about the normally disdainful task of squeezing into the dreaded corset. After scrubbing her face until it shone, she peered into the small looking glass and swiftly piled the mass of red curls securely into place.

She half expected to meet Sophia in the hall on her way out, but apparently her sister was still sleeping. *Oh, let her,* Lydia thought. *She could use the extra rest.*

Taking the steps two at a time, she burst into the small kitchen area, where her parents sat sipping cups of steaming coffee.

"Lydia, when will you learn to conduct yourself like a lady? You'd have thought there was a herd of elephants coming down the stairs." Her mother shook her head and took a delicate bite of the muffin in front of her.

"Good morning, Mother," Lydia responded affably. Even *she* was not going to get her down today. Pouring a large mug of coffee for herself, she turned and faced her parents.

"So. . ." She caught her father's eye and smiled. "Everything set, Dad?" She knew the answer already.

He glanced at his pocket watch, then met her gaze. "I think

so." He took another swig of the hot beverage as Lydia kept her smirk well hidden behind her own cup. "I imagine it wouldn't hurt to open a bit early—it being the first day and all."

Nodding her agreement, Lydia plopped down her half-drunk coffee and proceeded to follow him through the connecting door.

She loved seeing him like this. Ever eager and excited. A new venture.

"Lydia," her mother's voice stopped her. "Is Sophia up yet?"

"I. . .I think so." She glanced toward the ceiling. It wasn't a complete lie. She had heard some pattering around a couple minutes ago.

"I hope so. We can't be sleeping the day away with this store to keep. You'd do well to remember that, too."

Lydia nodded, brushed off her last comment, and hurried after her father, who was already turning around the "Open" sign. Racing to the door ahead of him, she unlatched the bolt and threw it open to usher in the fresh morning air along with their first customer.

A small boy of no more than five looked up at her with wide eyes. "Do ya sell penny candy here?"

Lydia smiled indulgently and stepped aside to let him in. "We sure do, sir! Right this way." She and her father exchanged chuckles. The day was starting well.

❧

The noon hour passed before the last of a steady stream of customers finally left. Lydia pushed an errant curl off her damp forehead. The day was hot already and promising to get worse.

Turning around and leaning against the counter, she watched her sister carefully recording figures in the thick ledger. She grimaced and was thankful that her job lay in restocking the shelves and dealing with customers. She'd never had a head for numbers.

Sophia set down her pen and pressed the newest entries with the blotter. A whoosh of breath sent her wispy blond hair up off her face. She swivelled on her stool and met Lydia's stare. "Some lemonade sound good to you?"

"Sounds great. In fact, a sandwich would taste pretty good about now, too." Her rumbling stomach reminded her that it was past dinnertime.

"Absolutely. I'm starved," Sophia concurred.

"You go ahead and eat first. I'll hang on in here until you're done."

A smiled thank-you was interrupted by the tapping of footsteps through the store's entrance. Lydia watched Sophia's face drain of color and just as quickly turn rosy pink. She swung around to meet a familiar pair of laughing blue eyes. "Well, Dr. Foy. How good of you to stop by."

"Good day, Miss Bennet." A playful smile twitched beneath his well-trimmed black mustache. "I hope your day has been productive."

"It has. Thank you. In fact, we—" She glanced back at her sister, who hadn't changed position during the whole exchange. "*I* was just about to break for my lunch. I'm sure that Sophia would be happy to help you."

Lydia headed toward the door, ignoring her older sister's momentary look of panic. "Have a nice day, Doctor."

"And you" came from over her shoulder.

She smiled as she passed through the doorway, hearing her sister's unmistakably soft and nervous voice that held a telltale touch of excitement.

A good ten minutes later, Sophia came through the door and paused. Lydia calmly kept eating her sandwich while perusing one of the newspapers her father had purchased in Veteran. She shoved the plate holding the sandwiches she'd made toward her sister, all the while keeping her gaze glued to the paper. "Hungry?"

Sophia took a seat opposite her at the table and promptly proceeded to snatch the periodical out of Lydia's hands. "You are incorrigible!"

Lydia grinned back at the smiling eyes before her. "And you're infatuated!"

"Get back in that store while I eat," her elder sister commanded playfully.

Taking one last swallow of lemonade, Lydia giggled quietly and stepped out of the kitchen, leaving her sibling to her thoughts. This change in Sophia was like a breath of fresh air.

There were no customers so Lydia occupied herself with straightening up and cleaning the glass on the display cases. She was rewrapping some bolts of fabric that had been looked over by several of the townswomen when she heard the shuffle of footsteps behind her. Holding her position on the small step stool, she continued shoving the remaining remnants into their places on the high shelf. "I'll be with you in a minute."

Her task completed, she stepped down carefully and turned around to find herself staring right at an extremely broad chest. Blinking and stepping back in retreat, she lifted her gaze to meet a pair of golden brown eyes and a tanned face topped with slick, dark brown hair. She wasn't entirely sure if she gasped out loud—she certainly hoped not—but her internal reactions couldn't be ignored.

After an interminable pause, his gaze wandered around the store, and she realized she'd probably stood there gaping for an embarrassingly long period. Clearing her throat, she skittered back behind the safety of her counter. She managed to find her voice. "Can I help you?"

His nod was barely perceptible, but he didn't speak. He continued to stride around the store, studying the inventory. His movement was deliberate and continuous, stopping only briefly to look once at the rifle cartridges and another time at the lanterns.

Lydia fidgeted nervously. She'd already offered her assistance. Should she again? Maybe he hadn't heard—no, he'd nodded. This was curious. Everyone else that day had been fairly chatty, curious for information on this new family in town and happy for the convenience of their own store once again. But this fellow. . .

An awful thought struck her. What if this was a robbery?

They were out west and—

She struck down that idea before it had a chance to blossom. It was broad daylight, and any number of people could walk in at any time. He was probably just quiet.

"Lydia." Her father's voice from behind her startled her from her reverie.

"Good day, sir." Father voiced his greeting to the man who was nearing the counter now that his circling of the store was nearly complete.

Again, the stranger nodded.

"Mighty hot today," her father ventured.

Another incline of the dark head. "It is at that."

Lydia jerked her head up at the comment. His voice held a strange raspy quality to it. Wait! He sounded just like that man from the back of the school house last Saturday night.

Her father had crossed around the counter and was now speaking with the man near the ammunition shelves. Their voices were quieter, but she was sure this man was indeed the same gentleman she'd heard the other night.

She busied herself with idle, pointless jobs just to hear their conversation.

"Just up from Independence," her father was sharing. "Sure is pretty country up here. Are you from these parts?"

"Originally."

"So, you've traveled about then?"

"Here and there."

Lydia smiled. Her father's talkative, outgoing nature wasn't getting too much out of this one. She noticed they were headed back toward her, so she stepped over to the register to ring up the purchases.

The man slid a couple dozen cartridges across the wooden surface. Her face must have betrayed her surprise at the number, and she felt him looking at her.

He shrugged his shoulders. "Habit, I guess," he simply stated.

"Is there anything else we can get for you, Mr. . ." Her father's voice trailed off.

"Jonas," he finished for him. "Caleb Jonas."

"John Bennet." Her father shook his hand. "This is Lydia." He nodded toward her. She smiled politely as she placed his items in a paper sack.

Jonas tipped his head ever so slightly. "Hope you enjoy Darby, Mrs. Bennet."

Lydia's face flushed, and she floundered for a response.

Her father chuckled. "*Miss* Bennet," he corrected their customer. "My wife is down to the post office. This is my daughter."

Those brown eyes seemed to assess her somewhat differently, and a hint of a smile turned up the corners of his lips. She squared her shoulders and tried to meet his unnerving gaze. Just when she thought she might have conquered that odd feeling in her stomach and that undefined challenge in his eyes, he looked away.

"Don't see any liquor here," Jonas stated, scanning the room one more time.

"No," her father volunteered. "I figure the saloon has plenty of that. I'll sell some for medicinal purposes, but other than that, I can't say I'm much in favor of it. Sorry."

"No apology necessary." He scooped up his bag from the stand. "Don't touch the stuff anymore anyway. Just noticed it wasn't around."

"I see. Well, we'll hope to see you again, Mr. Jonas."

"I'm sure you will." He smiled more openly now at her father. "Good day, *Miss* Bennet." With that, he turned and walked directly out of the store and into the street, leaving Lydia to wonder where she'd heard his name before.

❧

Supper that evening was a flurry of conversation. The first day had gone well. Even Mother seemed in good spirits. "I daresay, we may fare well here if our days are half as busy as this one has been."

Lydia's father nodded enthusiastically. "And the folks here seem real friendly." He appeared to consider that thought as he forked up a piece of roast beef. "I think we'll like it here."

Sophia didn't contribute much to the conversation but alternately toyed with her food and looked out the window.

"Well, I think I heard a good deal of news at the post office," her mother was continuing. "It seems that's the place to hear what's what and who's whom."

Lydia rolled her eyes and prepared to tune out the latest gossip. It couldn't be starting already.

"Quite a number of ranchers around the area will be making the trip to our store as well, according to Mrs. Carson, the postmistress. But it sounds as though the biggest one is the Box CJ Ranch, a good distance north. Some fellow named Jonas or something."

Lydia's head popped up.

"Ah, I think we met him in the store this afternoon," her father offered.

"Really?" Her mother's eyebrows raised. "It seems he's something of an enigma in this region."

"Hm. Sounded from him like he was from here."

Lydia watched the volley of conversation between her parents, holding her breath.

"Apparently he was. But his family was killed when he was quite young. Then he took off about ten years ago, and no one is entirely certain where he was or what he did during that time. He's just been back the last two or three years."

"Hm."

Lydia pushed back her chair. "Could I be excused, please?"

"I think I'm done as well," Sophia agreed.

Their mother looked at their plates. "Neither of you ate much of anything."

"Oh, just the excitement of the day, I guess," Lydia offered and looked at her sister.

"You do both look a trifle tired," their father noticed.

"Very well," Mrs. Bennet consented. "We'll see you in the morning."

Lydia hastily cleared her dishes and headed up the stairs. Once in the confines of their room, she shimmied out of her dress and unlaced her corset with a breath of relief. She heard

Sophia performing the same task.

"Busy day," Lydia commented.

"Um hm."

A smile crossed Lydia's lips. She knew where her sister's thoughts were. Ah, well. She'd leave her to them. She had her own thoughts to unscramble.

After pulling on her nightdress, Lydia crossed to her bed and lifted up the mattress. Lying snugly against the ropes was her coveted friend and confidant when she was in moods such as these. She plucked up the myriad of papers she called her journal and the pencil lying near it.

Flopping down on her bed, she faced the window and studied the fading vision of the North Platte. Where to start? Her day had entailed so much. So many people, experiences, emotions. But in spite of it all, one vision stayed firmly planted in her mind: a lean, dark face, light brown eyes framed by a dark, brooding brow. . .

She tapped the pencil against her teeth, then bent her head down and began to write.

six

The next several weeks established a new pattern for the Bennet household. The mercantile was doing well, and soon Lydia found her mind wandering as she completed her repetitive tasks. But worse yet, the newness of the store and Darby itself was already wearing off.

She convinced herself that fresh experiences, even minor ones, would keep feelings of boredom at bay. More often than not, on a Saturday evening, her attention would be drawn down the street to the schoolhouse. But she could only imagine what going to a social dance was like. Her mother had always made it quite clear that respectable persons did not take part in such worldly pursuits. There was bound to be revelry brought about by liquor.

Days that droned into monotony seemed to revive the ever-present friction between Lydia and her mother. Every aspect from clothes to hair to curfew hours were volleyed back and forth between two equally unyielding players.

One Saturday, the fray actually did begin over the evening's social at the schoolhouse—but through quite an unexpected medium.

Lydia and Sophia pushed through their normal afternoon routine, with Sophia bent over the ledger and Lydia rearranging a few shelves of fabrics and straightening the canisters along the back wall. Their mother, with practiced ease and decorum, bustled about helping the intermittent customer.

At the sound of another set of footsteps entering the store, Lydia watched her mother pause momentarily before descending upon the newest visitor. "Good day, sir," she fairly gushed.

Lydia turned to see who would illicit such an eager greeting. She momentarily caught her breath when a pair of dark eyes peered out from under the brim of a black Stetson. With unaccountable nervousness, she whirled back around and quickly sought something to keep her busy.

"Good day, ma'am."

"Is there something I might do for you, Mr. Jonas?"

Lydia, her back still turned, noted the hesitation before he spoke. "I see you know who I am, Mrs. Bennet. Pleased to make your acquaintance officially."

"Oh. . .well. . ."

Lydia bit back a smug smile at her mother's faux pas. She *couldn't* have known who he was—unless she'd been somewhere she had *heard* about him.

He chuckled slightly. "No matter. I think I'd have been a might surprised if you *hadn't* heard of me by now."

Lydia kept herself busy as the conversation turned to a discussion of available supplies. But while Mr. Jonas remained in the store, she listened intently to his distinctive, husky voice.

After he'd collected his purchases, her mother approached the till and began to add them up. Torn between disappointment and relief, Lydia casually made her way toward the front counter, keeping up her task at hand.

"If you don't mind my mentioning, Mr. Jonas," her mother started. "My husband told me that you remarked about our lack of liquor."

"Yep. No matter though. That's one demon I'm shut of."

"Well, good for you, Mr. Jonas. It takes strong character to stand up for what's right."

"Oh, I wouldn't jump to any fast conclusions about my convictions, ma'am. If it weren't for the simple fact that it nearly killed me, I'd probably be imbibing it today."

Lydia slowly turned, catching his eye.

He nodded in greeting.

"You don't say!" her mother pressed.

Lydia tried not to grimace. She hoped her mother wouldn't go into any sermonizing.

"Well," he clarified with a sheepish smile. "I can't blame the drink altogether. A lot of it was youth and simple stupidity."

The eagerness on her mother's face shone plainly as she leaned over, waiting for the remainder of the tale.

Aghast at such shocking behavior, Lydia shifted uncomfortably from one foot to the other, then finally removed herself from the background and continued to the other side of the shop. She'd be the last to admit she was just as curious to hear more details.

He picked up his sacks full of belongings and grinned. "Have a nice afternoon, ma'am." With a jaunty bow of his head, he turned to exit the store, leaving her mother to only imagine the end of the story.

He managed to steal past Lydia on his way out, a definite twinkle in his eye. "Spotless counters. I'll have to try one of those to shine up my saddle." He grinned impishly as his eyes fell to her hands.

She followed his gaze and smothered a gasp of mortification. There, crumpled and snagged, was one of the dainty lace handkerchiefs they sold. She wadded it up and stuffed it behind her on the shelf. But before she could return his look or his comment, he'd gone.

The rest of the afternoon rushed by in a blur. Trying to forget the latter part of the encounter, Lydia kept replaying the conversation Mr. Jonas had had with her mother. When her mother mentioned that the townspeople thought of him as some sort of mystery, Lydia had assumed him to be an arrogant, well-to-do chump trying to exaggerate his own charm. But his charm, feigned or not, was definitely beginning to have an effect on her. And that puzzled her.

More than once she'd caught herself surmising something or other about him, then would quickly cut off her thoughts. She didn't even know this man. Chalking it up to the "naive city girl comes west" mentality, she tried to shake it from her mind.

Just before closing time, Lydia's mother turned to her. "Lydia, would you go and finish getting supper on. Sophia and I will finish up in here."

Grateful to be alone with her tumbling thoughts, Lydia strode into the kitchen and began setting the table. She was vaguely aware of someone entering the store and the ensuing chatter but didn't pay it much mind.

Several minutes later, a red-eyed Sophia bustled through the door and scampered upstairs. Lydia didn't have a chance to voice any concern before her mother entered. Her face was drawn and flushed, the leftover glints of anger charging her blue eyes.

"Don't even start," she warned, shaking a finger.

Lydia widened her eyes and spun around to finish setting the table. She definitely didn't need another go-around with her mother. But it was odd, though, that the problem stemmed from Sophia—the trouble-free child.

Following Father's arrival home from meetings with other business owners, supper came and went—albeit without Sophia's presence. Not a word was uttered throughout the meal, and Lydia shifted anxiously in her seat, eager to check on her older sister.

Her father's inquiry finally loosed the dam. "Is Sophia not feeling well this evening?"

"She's fine." Her mother calmly forked her last bite of pie into her mouth.

Interminable silence.

"Just not hungry?" her father urged.

"Nothing significant, John. Merely a need to clarify our position on certain matters."

Lydia was convinced her father's muddled expression must have matched her own.

Her mother sighed in impatience. "Dr. Foy came in this afternoon just before closing."

"Ah, a fine man," her father interjected.

"Yes, quite. Anyway, he had the misguided notion that Sophia might wish to accompany him to the. . .the social this evening." The last phrase came out with utter disdain.

Lydia felt a lump rise in her throat.

"And she didn't?" Mr. Bennet asked.

"Well. . .I can't say. That's entirely beside the point, John. Sophia knows full well that we don't condone such behavior. To be truthful, I was surprised to hear that *he* would attend."

Lydia was torn between the desire to rush upstairs and comfort her broken sister and the temptation to berate her mother's insensitivity. Her feelings boiled very near the surface.

Her father's face held a troubled look as he toyed absently with the spoon near his coffee cup. "Do you think there's all that much to be concerned about?"

A look of sheer exasperation covered her mother's face. "For pity's sake! There you go again! Always have to have your hand in meddling where things that needn't concern you. I'm putting forth considerable effort to raise proper young *ladies* here, not a couple foolhardy, sow-their-wild-oats boys!"

"Like me?"

Lydia flinched in surprise at her father's uncharacteristic retort.

Her mother must have been equally shocked, for she remained silent.

"Mary, I understand your point of view, but I think you carry it a little far at times. There is nothing inherently evil about citizens getting together to swap laughter and good times. It's not as if the affair is held in a saloon, you know. It's a school—a church!"

"Not on those nights, I daresay!"

Father opened his mouth as though to say something, then resolutely clamped it shut. He directed a penetrating look toward her. "Would you please excuse your mother and me for a while, Lydia?"

Needing no further encouragement, she bolted upstairs just before the tense voices floated up after her. It was tempting to slam the door on the whole ordeal, but she was able to maintain some control and shut it gently.

Sophia lay on her bed, her eyes fixed on some indefinite point on the ceiling.

"Sophia?" Lydia gently inquired. "Do you want to talk?"

A simple head shake.

As the conversation below raised and lowered, Lydia found herself unable to control her desire to escape. How on earth her sister could simply lie there taking it all in was beyond her.

Some silly notion within her had her thinking that these times might lessen after their move. Foolish assumption. Especially when her mother had not been entirely thrilled to relocate.

Vacillating between pacing the creaky floorboards and sitting for several seconds on her bed, Lydia listened as the controversy downstairs began shifting. Not so amazingly, her name could be ascertained from the muffled spat. A sure sign. At any moment her mother would be heading up the stairs to administer one of her talks.

A quick glance at Sophia revealed she'd finally given into sleep, a momentary respite from her troubled heart.

But where could *she* go?

A sudden summer breeze blew through the window, carrying with it the unmistakable scent of the night-cooled river. Without a second thought, Lydia headed out of her room. At the end of the hall was a door that must at one time have opened onto an elevated porch. Praying it was accessible, she spun around and snatched her journal from beneath her ticking.

Her hasty footsteps brought her to the promised portal. She grasped the worn knob and tugged with all her might. Groaning under the pressure, the hinges finally relented and allowed her passage.

She took a deep breath as she surveyed the sudden drop at her feet. Funny, the building didn't seem nearly this high from the ground. Undaunted, she clenched her journal tightly between her teeth and leaned across the several feet it took for her hand to grasp the nearest branch of the aging cottonwood.

Deftly she shinnied down toward the trunk and dropped to the ground. Hiking up her cumbersome skirts, she dashed to the river and flopped with a relieved sigh on the dew-covered bank.

Closing her eyes and taking in a renewing breath of the night's air, she withdrew her pencil from the banded journal and flipped it open to a clean page. After thinking for a moment, she began writing.

If the moon came from the mountain tops
and illumined the rocky land
There'd be a man with a Stetson and a Winchester
who'd crossed many a sand

A lean hard face, full of pride
darkened by the sun
A nomadic life of travel
always on the run

Yet eyes so soft and caring
and his touch like a gentle breeze

Lydia balked at her own words on the page before her. She hadn't a clue about this fellow—much less cause to be thinking of him in any sort of amorous. . .

She furiously scribbled out the offending words and began a new phrase.

As a gentleman, he may fall in love
but then you'd find him gone
For his life is lived a day at a time
and his best friend is the dawn

Musing on her last sentiments, she tried to reason out what she had written. Again, she reflected that she didn't know a whit about Caleb Jonas. But why was it that she felt she did? One glance into his dark eyes seemed to speak volumes to her soul. Why? Was there some common thread between them—something her soul recognized but her intellect couldn't fathom?

If I had but one chance
to meet the mountain's son
I think I'd fall in love
and join him in his run.

Much sooner than she'd anticipated, the air began its steady cooling. The latter part of night was coming fast, and as much as she hated to end her evening here, Lydia knew she would have to get home soon.

With a breath of resignation, she ambled back to the store. By now, she was sure that her trail of evidence had followed her. Oh, well. At least she'd had a bit of time away.

True to expectation, her mother was sitting at the table when Lydia made her appearance in the kitchen. Father was nowhere to be seen, and she assumed he'd turned in for the evening.

Steeling herself for the onslaught, Lydia stood in her place, waiting for the inevitable. Several moments ticked by in unaccustomed silence.

Her mother finally took one last sip of tea before rising and placing her dishes in the wash basin. When she returned to the table, she picked up a small pamphlet and handed it across the table.

"Read it," her mother admonished. "And prepare yourself. I believe we may have delayed this action far too long already." She ushered herself out of the room and up the stairs, leaving Lydia alone.

Lydia stared at the pamphlet, transfixed. Across the front in bold lettering were the words *St. Augustine's Ladies College.*

seven

Whether it was the threat of the stuffy ladies' college or merely the good weather and increased clientele, Lydia and her mother managed to avoid any major confrontations for the next few weeks. But Sophia's complexion had once again grown inordinately pale, and this time Lydia knew why.

The only time the bloom returned to Sophia's face was when a certain doctor graced the door of their establishment. In spite of Sophia's inability to accept his previous invitation, he still frequented the store and seemed not to harbor any bitterness toward her. If anything, his countenance seemed even softer and more gentle than it had been previously. Lydia surmised that he'd pieced together the situation with their mother. But numerous attempts to convince Sophia of this brought a simple shrug of her shoulders and resolute silence.

Anyway, Lydia was faced with her own set of struggles. It had been some weeks since that highly embarrassing encounter with Mr. Jonas. Each time the bell rang above the door, part of her breathed in relief that the incoming customers didn't include the mystery man. Yet another side had her intently listening for any news regarding the Box CJ Ranch and its elusive owner.

One particularly sultry June afternoon, Lydia had just finished stuffing the last of the bills and coins Sophia had counted out the evening before into a money bag. It was time for their first trip to the bank, since the banker had been out of town and had only returned a day or two ago.

Lydia had rather enjoyed these outings while in Independence and looked forward to it again here. She dressed in one of her frillier gowns, complete with bustle, pinned her hat upon her curls, and took to the boardwalk. The bank was located on the opposite side of the main street, farther down toward the school. By now, several faces were familiar to her, and she waved back in greeting as she crossed the dry, dusty street.

The bank's heavy door was propped open to let in some fresh, if not cool, air. Lydia stepped into the dim room, waiting for her eyes to adjust.

A shuffle of papers and a deep-voiced "Be with you in a moment" acknowledged her presence.

She glanced around the goodly sized room and noted with some surprise the lavishness of its decor. This certainly didn't look like a bank that belonged in Darby. It didn't even look like the bank in Independence. This would do well in some city back east. As she continued her perusal of the velvet-covered chairs, the shiny mahogany desks, and the rich tapestries gracing the walls, she became aware of a presence by her side.

Startled, she stepped back and looked up into the smiling young stranger's face. His fair complexion, a definite oddity in this region, stood in contrast to his light brown hair and eyes. "Good afternoon, Miss Bennet." He graciously took her hand and made a semiformal bow. "I'm pleased to finally make your acquaintance. I've heard nothing but good things about your family's enterprise since my return."

Still stunned by this man's gentility, she merely smiled back.

"Come," he took her arm, led her to an expansive and meticulously neat desk, and offered her a chair. As he stepped behind the heavy piece of furniture, she noted that his apparel did justice to the rest of his surroundings. Under his satiny vest was a crisp white stiff-collared shirt set off by a rich burgundy ascot, complete with a jeweled stick pin. Hanging from his vest pocket, a glistening gold chain assured the presence of a pricey pocket watch. Even his mustache and pointed cheek whiskers spelled out obvious wealth.

Lydia wasn't sure whether to feel intimidated. Having been raised the daughter of a merchant, they'd rarely lacked for anything. But she got the distinct impression that their earnings would be meager next to this man's.

He clasped his hands together in front of him and rested them on the desk. "So you're here to start your family's account." He reached into a drawer and pulled a small number of papers. "Your father spoke with me before I left town and I—" He looked up suddenly and gave her a rather indulgent smile. "Do forgive me, Miss Bennet. I just realized you don't even know who I am."

He reached across and offered his hand again, not shaking hers, as was so often the custom here, but tenderly grasping it in almost reverence. "Bradley Smyth, at your service."

Lydia felt her face flame under his glimmering eyes, and she abruptly withdrew her hand.

"Thank you, Mr. Smyth. I know my father has informed you of our situation. I trust that the two of you have all the details worked out."

Sliding the papers over to her, he nodded. "All that's needed, Miss Bennet, is for you to sign here to verify it was you who brought the currency in today." He indicated with his finger, and Lydia noted the smoothness of his hand.

Taking up the offered pen, she dipped it into a nearby inkwell and signed her name. "I'm glad that's all I have to do," she laughed. "I'm afraid I'm inexperienced in such matters as ledgers and receipts."

"Well, now," he mused. "One with such beauty ought not need to trouble her pretty head with numbers."

Involuntarily stiffening, she stood brusquely and placed the money bag on his desk. Not sure whether to feel incensed at his comment, she busied her hands with straightening the lace on her sleeve. "If you'll excuse me, Mr. Smyth. I'm needed back at the store."

"Of course. It just so happens that I must make a trip to your business anyway. Might I have the pleasure of escorting you home?"

Lydia smothered a resigned sigh. It was far too soon for her to have framed any sort of opinion of this man, much less an uncharitable one.

She glanced up into his comely face. "Very well," she

agreed and waited patiently while he slipped on his long, pin-striped sack coat and placed his derby on his wavy brown hair.

"Shall we be off?" He smiled generously and led her out the door, straight into a near collision with a pair of leviathan shoulders and a black Stetson.

Lydia gasped and found herself being steadied on one arm by the banker and on the other by a stronger, more rugged grasp. She quickly regained her footing, but neither grip loosened on her arms. She suppressed the urge to giggle as she stood feeling akin to a wishbone.

She glanced first at the dark face to her right. "Thank you, Mr. Jonas. I'm quite alright." His puzzled face held a slightly questioning look as he directed his gaze at her companion. Then, as if suddenly realizing himself, he released her.

A look to Mr. Smyth's side revealed his already light complexion blanching further by the minute. She frowned in curiosity.

Several seconds later, the banker found his voice. "Shall we continue on, Miss Bennet?" Without waiting for an answer, he tugged her gently after him down the walk.

She glanced over her shoulder to see Caleb Jonas still looking after them with a contemplative frown across his dark brows.

❧

Lydia eagerly shimmied out of her confining dress and corset and slipped on her soft cotton nightdress. Quickly rinsing her face in the basin, she blotted herself dry and began to unpin her mass of curls.

Sophia had long since finished with her task and was sitting quietly on her bed, running a brush through her fine, blond hair. She was quietly humming a lilting melody as she stared out the window above her bed.

Grasping a memory from a few years back, Lydia approached her sister's bed and held out her hand for the brush. Sophia smiled up at her, obviously remembering as well, and relinquished it.

Lydia plopped behind her on the ticking and proceeded to carefully pull the bristles through her sister's silky tresses. "What are you thinking?" She started the age-old game they'd been playing since they were five or six years old. Over the years their answers had changed from dreams of castles and fairy princesses to stolen glances at a certain someone and dreams for the future.

It had been their special time until a couple years ago. For some reason, still unknown to Lydia, Sophia had quit sharing. Now, Lydia would try again.

She kept brushing, waiting to see if an answer would come.

After several minutes, she'd resigned herself to the fact that Sophia just wasn't going to open up. But she continued her task anyway.

"He was in again today."

Lydia nearly dropped the silver handle in shock. She caught her sister's arm and spun her around to face her. "Dr. Foy?"

An eager nod.

"And?" she prompted.

"He's asked me to go riding with him this Sunday next. To take a picnic on the Platte." Sophia's light blue eyes sparkled as her lips quivered in a bashful smile.

Lydia enveloped her in a squeeze. "See? I told you! And you were so worried."

Her sister nodded shyly and looked at her hands. "I'm a little bit scared, Lydia."

"Oh, hush. You'll be fine. Just be yourself. You've a tremendous sense of humor when you open up. He'll—"

"I don't mean that," Sophia interrupted.

Lydia cocked her head to one side in curiosity. "Well, then, what *do* you mean?"

Her sister's slender fingers began toying with the drawstrings of her gown. "It's just that. . .I don't know. I guess I'm just afraid that—"

"Lydia!" Their mother's voice resounded up the stairs.

Lydia rolled her eyes. Grasping Sophia's tiny hands, she

looked her straight in the eyes. "Whatever it is, don't worry about it, Sissy. I'm just sure this is going to work out. Okay?"

She nodded with a brave smile.

Lydia gave her a quick kiss on the forehead and, standing up, steeled herself for whatever lay waiting downstairs.

Stepping off the stairs into the kitchen, she heard muffled voices coming from the parlor. At least both her parents waited for her. It couldn't be too serious.

She walked down the short hall to the more formal room and found the pair perusing several periodicals. Her mother glanced up and greeted her with a smile.

"Come in and sit down, Lydia, dear." She motioned to the settee with her hand.

Lydia, still cautious, perched on the edge and waited.

"I want to commend you on your deportment lately," her mother began. "It's been a vast improvement, wouldn't you say, John?"

Her father looked up from his paper with an understanding smile at Lydia. "Yes, I guess I'd say so."

"Well, I just want to let you know that our presentation of St. Augustine's may have been a trifle premature."

Lydia was more than a little confused. She took a deep breath as she waited for her mother to continue.

"We thought it would be best to let you know that Mr. Smyth spoke with your father and me after he escorted you home today." Her mother's face held a palpable gaiety.

Lydia nodded. She knew that much.

"He's a fine young man, don't you agree, John?" Her mother's gaze returned to her father's once again.

Lydia was growing impatient.

"He's from the East, you know," she informed Lydia. "Boston. He comes from a very prominent family. It seems he's picked up his business from his father. He was relating that he has several brothers who also. . ."

Lydia shifted in her seat and let her attention wander from her mother's words. Why on earth was she reporting all of this? He was certainly nothing to—

A horrendous thought flickered through Lydia's mind. Her mother couldn't be alluding to some sort of. . . No. It was too ridiculous. She'd only just met this man today. Slowly, her ears picked up the remainder of the monologue.

"And he's done quite well since coming to Darby, even though it's been only three years and considering the size of the town and the surrounding area.

"In any case, he's brought with him his proper manners and has asked your father and me if he might call on you in the future."

There. The dreaded words had been said. Lydia shook her head slowly, thinking surely she hadn't heard correctly.

Knowing a response was expected of her, she lifted her eyes to her mother's glowing face. "What did you tell him?"

Her mother's brow furrowed. "I told him that we'd be more than pleased to have our daughter associating with a gentleman of such refined character."

"I see." She squelched the desire to release an exasperated breath. Well, she shouldn't have been too surprised. Mr. Smyth was definitely what her mother would consider appropriate courting material. For now she'd just have to bide her time and think up some creative excuses for when he actually came to call.

If only a certain other gentleman had made his presence known to her parents. . . She pushed the thought aside. A quick recollection of that night behind the school reminded her that in all probability his attentions were engaged elsewhere. She hadn't wanted to face that fact. It wasn't part of her dream.

But what was going on here and now wasn't a dream either. It was all too real.

Just as Lydia was about to voice her opinion on the whole matter, she heard her mother's final statement: "He's asked to take you riding this Sunday after services. I told him you'd be honored to accompany him."

eight

Sunday loomed ever nearer. Lydia watched her sister's increasing anticipation of the day while she, herself, relished the upcoming event with as much enthusiasm as one about to face a firing squad. But one spark of news had lessened her apprehensions. These "drives" she and Sophia were taking to the North Platte would not be completely solitary. The whole town and people from the surrounding areas were to be there—a community affair, of sorts.

More than once she caught herself wondering if any ranchers might attend—one in particular. But then again came the remembrance of their last encounter. Odd, the way these thoughts insisted on tearing back and forth within her: half of her hoping against hope to see the man and the other half dreading any sort of meeting with him. She tried her best to put the issue from her mind.

All too soon, Sunday dawned. A blazing sun tinted the edges of a few fluffy clouds holding little promise of rain within their pearly exteriors. Lydia tried to shake off her own gray mood in the face of her sister's sweet spirit that morning. She decided that Sophia's expectations were worth any amount of discomfort she, herself, might have to bear. Then she gave herself a mental shake. If she deemed riding to a picnic on the banks of the North Platte with a wealthy and comely banker so utterly distasteful, maybe she was as ungrateful and difficult as her mother often indicated.

Determined to quell any misgivings, Lydia concentrated on preparing herself for church. She'd inwardly chided herself that her thoughts as of late were not centered where they should have been while worshiping. Try as she might to blame that fact on recent events and distracting persons, she knew it was no one's fault but her own. She murmured a quick prayer of apology and added another for patience for the day ahead.

❧

The walk home after church seemed shorter than normal this day. Lydia had to suppress her laughter as, in an extreme role reversal, *she* actually had to almost run to keep up with *Sophia's* quick footsteps. "Wait up, Sis!" she panted as she shuffled her fashionable new boots faster along the dust-covered boardwalk.

A sheepish smile came over Sophia's shoulder as she halted to accommodate Lydia's tardiness. "Sorry."

Lydia grinned back at her. "No, you're not." But they made the remainder of the walk together.

"Do you think Mr. Jonas might come?" Sophia asked after a brief silence.

Lydia hoped she'd managed to quash her inward surprise before it showed on her face. She tried to shrug nonchalantly. "I don't know. Why?"

Her sister gave her a dubious smirk. "Why?" she repeated. But before any more questions could issue forth, Lydia promptly changed the subject.

"When is Dr. Foy coming by for you?" she asked as they rounded the corner of their storefront.

"Almost right away." Sophia cantered up the steps to the back door, the former topic of conversation apparently forgotten. "I must go freshen up and recheck my hair. And I'll need to fetch my parasol." She glanced up at the glaring sun, and Lydia followed her gaze, scrunching up her nose in disdain.

"I hate carrying that cumbersome thing around—"

The comment was interrupted by the approach of slow hoofbeats. Around the corner came a covered surrey, resplendent in its finery. Heavy fringe and costly upholstery heralded the news that this was no ordinary local rig. At the reins of two jet black horses sat Mr. Bradley Smyth, by no means lost in his carriage's luster. His Sunday suit made his everyday attire suffer in comparison. Lydia stared for a moment, forgetting that she was to be preparing to leave with the man.

He drew up to the steps and granted the sisters a dazzling smile, tipping his bowler with practiced ease. "Good afternoon, Misses Bennet. Fine day for a picnic."

Lydia felt her sister elbow her gently, and she took her leave from gawking. "Quite right, Mr. Smyth. If you'll excuse me for one moment, allow me to fetch my parasol?"

He nodded his assent, flashing another polished smile as he maintained control of the spirited team.

Once in the house, Lydia took the stairs two at a time—a task not easily managed in her frock full of layer upon layer of petticoats. As she snatched her ruffled umbrella, she found herself chuckling. This afternoon might not be so vexing. She couldn't ignore the fact that she was more than excited to be sitting atop such a fine carriage. And behind such a team.

With renewed hopefulness, she skittered down the steps, reining herself in just before exiting the door. "See you at the festivities, Sophia." She squeezed her sister's arm as she stepped past and smiled at the handsome face above her as he leaned over to assist her.

"Thank you, Mr. Smyth." Lydia settled herself comfortably on the plush seat. "Shall we be off?"

Nodding, he cast an appreciative eye over her. "You're quite a captivating young woman, Miss Bennet."

Lydia first stared in surprise, then shifted a tad uncomfortably under his sudden scrutiny. His brown eyes held an undefinable gleam that unnerved her. But his gaze returned to hers, and his face took on its previous genteel demeanor. "It will be my honor to be escorting you today."

Focusing her eyes ahead, she toyed with her gloves and parasol ruffle, a quiet sigh of relief escaping once the team started into motion. Granted, this courting business was new to her, but she determined to get over the feeling of unease that seemed to accompany it.

They rode in companionable silence for a distance. The day was turning out to be warmer than anticipated, and she was grateful for the meager shade her parasol provided. For mid-June, the temperatures were unaccountably warm, she'd been informed. She noted the thin clumps of grass were quickly losing the greenish hue they'd sported just a few weeks ago. It was dry, and a good rain would be welcomed. She just hoped it wouldn't come today.

Lydia noted the number of conveyances that surrounded them in all directions. It appeared everyone in Wyoming Territory was making an appearance. And, irritatingly enough, she couldn't shake that niggling feeling in her stomach at the possibility that Mr. Jonas might be there as well. He did live a good distance out, in the opposite direction. Perhaps with such a large ranch, he would be too busy for such events.

"Certainly seems to be a crowd," Mr. Smyth noted.

She nodded. "It's hard to believe there are this many people around here. You never see a crowd this size in town."

"The territory is booming. More new residents moving in all the time." He smiled almost to himself as he glanced at the crowd of people.

"Do you think we'll become a state?" she queried.

"Eventually, anyway. There are just too many people to expect it might stay a territory indefinitely."

She nodded in agreement. "They've already taken such major steps. I still can't believe that women can actually vote here." She was about to add how she felt this was only proper, but a disgruntled "Humph!" interrupted her thoughts.

"Nonsense." Mr. Smyth shook his head. "Utter nonsense. What kind of knowledge do women have of politics and government? I hardly see that law remaining on the books, especially if and when Wyoming achieves statehood."

Aghast at his bold opinion, Lydia frowned as she replayed his words. She knew her mother also disapproved of such changes, maintaining that only unladylike and discontented women caused such chaos. But surely there had to be a place for *some* involvement of the fairer gender, Lydia reasoned.

She opened her mouth to retort when the banker drew the team to a halt and stood to dismount from the carriage. She was surprised to find they had arrived at the picnic grounds. The end of their journey may have also brought the end to their conversation, but Mr. Smyth's views on women's suffrage would stay tucked in her memory, to be sure.

She took a moment to study the pristine meadow that had been selected for the day's event. In spite of the partially browning grasses, it was a beautiful place. The field was wide enough to accommodate such a gathering and had a perfect smattering of trees to provide shade for those less able to tolerate the blistering sun. And the river's ever-present calm waters completed the picture.

Mr. Smyth deftly collected the wicker picnic basket from the rear of the surrey and offered his arm. Lydia took it, somewhat hesitantly, as she perched her opened parasol over her opposite shoulder.

It seemed everyone had come: town and farm and ranch folks alike. She offered waves to several business owners she recognized from town and fellow church members as well. Her eyes searched for any sight of her sister and the good doctor, but there were simply too many faces in the milling crowd. She did catch a glimpse of her parents near the shore of the wide river where several small rowboats were beached.

She had to smile at the sight. It was obvious that her father wanted to try his arm at a row around the calm water, but her mother stood resolutely shaking her head, her mouth moving faster than Lydia could decipher. She shook her head with a soft chuckle.

"What is it?"

She glanced up at her escort and nodded toward the dinghies.

"Would you care for a ride?"

"Oh!" She hadn't meant him to take it that way. Biting her lip in indecision, she looked up at him once more. Then again, a row over the gentle waves might be a lark. She nodded eagerly.

"Very well." His white teeth shone in his resolute smile and he headed her in the promised direction.

Once at the shore, Lydia fairly burst with excitement. She stood, shifting from one foot to the other in controlled impatience as her escort readied the boat. She'd never been in a rowboat before.

After setting their lunch basket into the bottom, he lent her a steady hand, and she stepped into the small vessel and took the proffered seat. He followed and nodded to the youngster whose job was to shove the crafts into the current, saving skirts and spats alike from exposure to the brownish water.

A quiet giggle escaped Lydia's lips as the dory slid through the water and shifted ever so slightly in the afternoon breeze. Glancing at Mr. Smyth, she found him giving her a pleased look. For one rare moment, she almost felt shy.

When he proceeded to remove his sack coat, she was unsuccessful in smothering a little gasp. Now it was his turn to chuckle. "It would be a bit difficult to manage the oars with this on." He smiled good-naturedly as he handed her the discarded article. "You'll notice the other gentleman have removed their outerwear as well."

Lydia glanced around and found he was right. She laughed at her own expense, draped the dark coat over her lap, and sat back to enjoy the ride. Across the placid water came the mingled sound of birds, soft laughter, and the periodic quiet splash of an oar piercing the water. Pulling off her lacy gloves, she leaned over and let her fingers trail in the tepid water, imagining how glorious it would feel to be taking a swim, unencumbered by a restrictive corset or heavy skirts, a thought that warmed her face. Bathing wasn't something that was done in mixed company, and the very idea of it made her blush.

Her reverie was interrupted by a sharp voice, closer than she would have expected. "Well, good afternoon, Mr. Smyth."

Lydia bolted upright and turned to look at the bearer of the greeting. A withering feeling went through her when she found herself perilously close to a boat carrying Miss Priscilla Davis. "And a good day to you, Miss Davis." Bradley Smyth tipped his hat, while Lydia managed a polite smile. She'd only met up with Priscilla Davis on two formal occasions in town, other than that night behind the schoolhouse. And that time she hadn't known who the young woman was. But now she was keenly aware that Priscilla's family was one of the more well-to-do in town, her father owning the local hotel and boarding house.

The raven-haired girl cast a simpering smile at Lydia. "Miss Bennet." Her blue eyes regarded Lydia coolly in spite of the pasted-on smile she wore.

Lydia had always felt and sensed an undercurrent of rivalry from Priscilla Davis. Today would have probably been no different were it not for the simple fact that the other girl's eyes were glued on the banker. Lydia smiled to herself. Priscilla was downright jealous.

Someone cleared his throat, breaking the silence. Priscilla was the first to speak. "I'm sure you both know my companion. . ."

Lydia adjusted the position of her parasol so it no longer blocked the remainder of the parallel vessel from view, anticipating the introduction. A pair of dark eyes, twinkling impishly, locked with hers. Instantly her stomach roiled into several knots.

"Mr. Caleb Jonas."

As the two men exchanged courtesies, Lydia earnestly concentrated on not losing the light breakfast she'd eaten that morning.

"Are you feeling well, Miss Bennet? Your face is positively white." Priscilla seemed to take joy in Lydia's discomfort.

Resolving to gather herself together, Lydia took several deep breaths. "Quite alright," she informed them, more shakily than she would have liked. "My first time in a rowboat, that's all."

"Oh," snickered Priscilla. "Guess I wouldn't know about that. Why, I've fairly grown up on this river. Some of us are more used to the way of life in a territory. What a pity, though. You'll miss the games." She turned her attention back to Mr. Smyth in a look of mocking concern. "Perhaps you'll need to escort our poor *Lydia* home."

Lydia bristled at the sound of Priscilla using her first name. Her normal fire of resolve rekindled itself and she straightened up, looking Miss Davis squarely in the eye. "I quite assure you that I'm fine." She turned her attention back to Priscilla's escort, intense determination suppressing even the butterflies in her stomach caused by meeting his gaze. "You might want to keep an eye on *Priscilla* though," she added. "We wouldn't want her to callous her delicate hands."

Lydia grabbed the resting oar handles from the oarlocks and plopped them into the water rather unceremoniously, causing a small cascade of murky water to spray across the front of Priscilla Davis's formerly white dress. Tugging with all her might, Lydia maneuvered the boat hastily toward shore.

Her reward was Caleb's deep, throaty laughter.

❧

Lydia popped the last bite of biscuit into her mouth and dabbed her lips with the linen napkin. Mr. Smyth had been extremely quiet since their boat ride—no doubt because of her ridiculous display. She'd tried to apologize several times, but he'd merely brushed it aside, assuring her it wasn't necessary. He'd even laughed once about it, stating he'd been surprised, but not offended. She puzzled over his continued pensiveness though.

"Thank you for the delicious lunch." She folded the napkin and replaced it in the wicker basket.

"My pleasure." He smiled distractedly.

Lydia frowned but let her attention wander over to where a large group of people were gathering. "What's going on over there?" She nodded in the general direction.

"Hm?" He seemed to bring his thoughts back to the present.

She tried again. "Do you suppose they're starting the games?"

"Perhaps." He refolded his napkin and placed it on top of his nearly untouched meal. "Would you care to watch?"

"I'd love to."

As they neared the activities, Lydia could sense the excitement in the air. The throng was so thick it took some time to work their way to the front. Several men had discarded their coats and even their vests, standing only in their shirts—many of the shirts unbuttoned at the neck and with their sleeves rolled up, at that.

Her heart skipped several beats when she spied Caleb Jonas's glistening chestnut head in the group. Unaccountably, he found her face and gave her a bold smile. She tried to look away, and when she turned she noticed Jonas's action had not gone unseen by her companion. She watched in curiosity as his eyes narrowed slightly.

An older gentlemen stood before the gathering, lifting his arms above him to focus the group's attention, and raised his voice. "The foot race is about to begin. Any other competitors better come forward now. The race will start in just a few minutes."

Loud murmurs and laughter shuffled through the crowd. Some of the contestants even taunted others to join them. Lydia turned her attention back to the broad-shouldered rancher, who was talking to several of the other men and laughing jovially. Forgetting that one wasn't to stare, she took in his tall form and obviously muscular arms barely hidden by his partially opened shirt. At one point he turned in her direction and the sun fell across his face and neck in a brilliant beam. It was then that she saw it. A straight white scar formed a clean line across his neck, just below his throat. She heard herself gasp and quickly checked herself, glancing around to make certain no one else had heard her.

Returning her attention to Caleb, she studied the scar, and her mind began to take off on all sorts of fancies. Had he had his throat slit at knifepoint? Perhaps by an Indian? She recalled that there were many unconfirmed but interesting stories floating around about his past. Some reported that he'd lived with Indians, others said that he merely was captured by them as a prisoner, and yet others implied that he was wanted for any number of crimes further west. Which crime it was depended on who you talked to. In any case, she reasoned, there was no longer a mystery about why he had such a raspy voice.

Suddenly, he fixed his gaze upon her. Then on her companion. "Mr. Smyth," he called out. "Won't you join us?"

A hush fell on the persons around them, and Bradley

Smyth's fair complexion paled slightly before reddening. Regaining his composure astonishingly fast, he smiled rather indulgently. "Thank you, Mr. Jonas. But I think I'm much more needed here." He took a step closer to Lydia and firmly placed her arm in his. A few chuckles drifted about. Lydia stood, horrified at his forward gesture, but not knowing what to do. She watched Caleb's face for any troubled looks but saw none. He simply continued to smile.

"That's too bad," he continued. "If you run half as fast as you seem to accumulate and spend money, you might be a bit of a challenge for me."

That statement brought roars from the crowd, and Lydia had to stifle a smile. But when the arm holding hers stiffened, she averted her gaze to the ground.

After the laughter had died down, Smyth's voice came softly but firmly. "Miss Bennet, would you please excuse me for a few minutes?"

She looked up and nodded. Watching him walk off, she wondered if he needed some time to cool down.

"I see you're taking in the games after all," a voice from behind her stated.

Lydia rolled her eyes before turning to face the inevitable. But to her surprise, Priscilla Davis's face was unaccountably agreeable. She was even smiling.

Lydia glanced down at the bodice of the girl's gown. A few telltale brown spots still remained. She felt a flicker of remorse.

"I'm terribly sorry about your dress. I didn't mean to splash you like that." And it was true. She hadn't had any intentions of dousing the girl. She had simply intended to row away. How was she to know the oars would be so heavy?

"Oh, don't concern yourself," Priscilla assured her. "I've dozens. And I'm certain it will come out. The real reason I came over was to invite you to join me."

"Join you? In what?"

"The three-legged race."

Lydia scrutinized her expression carefully to see if she was joking, but Priscilla showed no indication of it.

"Really. The three-legged race?" She paused. "I assumed it was only the men who were competing today. I've never heard of women taking part—"

"Oh, of course!" Priscilla grabbed Lydia's arm and began to drag her from the crowd. "It's over in this area, come on!"

"But what about the foot race?"

"Oh, we'll hear who wins. Besides, we need to get ready." She continued to pull Lydia along behind her.

"Ready?"

"Well, sure. Do you think we'll run a three-legged race in these?" She laughed as she fingered her abundant skirts. "Of course not, silly. We wear trousers."

That stopped Lydia short. "Trousers!"

Priscilla turned and faced her, a trace of impatience on her face. "Yes, trousers. Everyone does it. Don't worry." She continued leading her toward a grassy area with a number of small buildings, presumably privies. "I've placed your outfit in here." She indicated to the closest building. "Mine's in that one." She pointed to the next one. "Jenny, come here!" Priscilla yelled to a girl standing not too far away. Lydia recognized her as Jenny Parker, another girl from town who usually kept company with Priscilla.

"Jenny will hold our dresses for us so they won't get dirty. Then we can change back into them after the race." Priscilla started to head in the direction of her appointed structure.

"Wait!" Lydia was getting a funny feeling from all of this.

Priscilla turned around.

"Are you sure you want me for your partner?"

"I guess that depends," Priscilla answered.

"On what?"

"Whether you think you can keep up with me or not."

Nothing else needed to be said. Lydia hiked her chin and started toward the waiting clothes. She'd show her who could keep up with whom.

nine

Caleb roamed around impatiently as he waited for the race to start. It seemed to him that they'd waited long enough already.

He cast a glance over to where he'd seen the Bennet girl, but she was no longer there. Nor was her escort. Shrugging his shoulders, he tried to push her winsome features from his mind. But he somehow couldn't help musing on why she might be attending the gathering with that stuffy banker of all people. Maybe she wasn't aware of some of the man's less-than-charitable traits. That had to be it.

Caleb, himself, had only recently been apprised of some news about the good Mr. Smyth which had some of his neighboring ranchers a trifle hot under the collar. Not that it was any concern of his, he reasoned. She could rightly choose whom she preferred to spend her time with.

A familiar black bowler caught his eye. Sure enough, it was Mr. Moneybags himself talking with some young man. When the person in question turned around, Caleb saw it was Kid Cooley, one of the local hooligans who, when he wasn't driving an occasional herd of cattle, was spending his earnings in the local saloon. Caleb didn't know much about him other than the fact that he considered himself something of a marksman with his pistol. A fact which had yet to be proven.

Before he knew it, the baby-faced Cooley was sauntering toward him, a sappy grin covering his ruddy features. Caleb issued a polite nod of recognition.

"Mr. Jonas." Everything about this kid smacked of reckless abandon. A smirk colored every word and facial expression. He was mighty pleased with himself, that was for certain. "Thought I might give you a bit of competition." He grinned and, his gray eyes never leaving Caleb's face, proceeded to spit tobacco juice just shy of Caleb's new shoes.

Fighting an uncontrollable urge to teach the pup a lesson, Caleb inwardly took a step back. Hadn't he dealt with enough interlopers during his time in Texas? Here was simply a kid whose britches were just a shade too big for him. Somebody would bring him down to size eventually. It didn't have to be his job.

Smiling evenly, Caleb kicked a small clod of dirt over the offending stain on the ground, leaving a trail of dust to settle on the young man's recently shined boots. "Better be careful there, son. Didn't your mama ever tell you that stuff's not good for you? You're liable to swallow it and make yourself terrible sick."

A scowl covered Kid Cooley's face as he surveyed the layer of earth covering his boots. "That wasn't very nice," he announced in a threatening tone.

"Neither is expectorating," Caleb volleyed back.

"Expect—what?"

Just then the man in charge of the race gave a shrill whistle to signal it was time to begin. Caleb turned and faced forward. The kid stuck right with him. "What was that supposed to mean?" his irritated voice pressed.

"Look, son." Caleb shot him a patronizing glance. "Give it up, will you? Apparently your upbringing involved a decided lack of education and manners. Why don't you concentrate on what you probably have had the most practice at?"

Kid Cooley, still somewhat puzzled, questioned him further. "And what's that?"

Caleb hunkered down in anticipation as he saw the starting pistol raise in the air. "Well. . .running with your tail between your legs, of course."

The deafening shot pierced through the air, and Caleb jumped ahead before he had an opportunity to observe Kid's reaction.

His mind fully on the race ahead of him, he paced himself, taking long, even strides over the unfamiliar and bumpy terrain.

He noted several other men had pulled ahead immediately, but gauging the distance of the determined course, he wasn't too worried. They'd be wrung out before they rounded the second stand of cottonwoods.

All along the designated route, groups of people yelled, cheered, and whistled as the runners continued on. Caleb normally let such a competition fully occupy his thoughts, but his mind kept taking unusual turns. . .namely wondering if a certain redhead was watching. Would she be clinging to that pompous Smyth's arm and rooting for Kid Cooley, who had obviously been sent in by Smyth to curtail any chance of Caleb's walking away with the prize money?

The distracting questions mingled with anger, confusion, pride, and his ever-present competitiveness. His second wind surged through his veins, and he picked up the pace. There was no way he would allow that arrogant Bradley Smyth to gloat over any loss of his, particularly with the storekeeper's daughter at his side.

Passing by several men, Caleb shot ahead, anticipating the last corner of the course around the great tent that had been set up in case of inclement weather. The last stretch was surprisingly effortless, and he flew across the finish line. Slowing down to a jog, he breathed in and out heavily, trying to catch his breath. *Jonas,* he mused with a chuckle, *you're gettin' too old for this.*

Hearty slaps on his back heralded his triumph, and he stood to accept the congratulations while more of the runners straggled in over the finish line, Kid Cooley among them. After reaching the end, the youngster leaned over, panting and wheezing almost uncontrollably.

Caleb grinned and strode to the disabled fellow. Clapping him on the back, perhaps a little harder than necessary, he bent down in feigned concern. "Maybe I was wrong back there, boy. It oughtn't be tobacco that you cut out. Looks like it should be cigarettes. I hear they're hard on a person's wind." He smiled as he caught the young man's icy glare. "Better luck next time." And he sauntered away whistling, passing right by the equally stony face of Bradley Smyth.

Caleb found a glass of lemonade to quench his thirst. It felt good going down his parched throat, but considering the still high sun, he began to wonder if pouring it directly over his head might offer more relief. He'd just finished the last swallow when a feminine voice spoke at his side. "Excellent race."

He turned to find Priscilla Davis gazing up at him with wide blue eyes.

"Thanks." He smiled and placed his empty glass on a nearby table. As he turned toward her again, he noted her demeanor held a palpable eagerness.

"Are you going to enter the next event?" she asked.

Frowning in curiosity, he answered, "I don't believe so. I'm still a bit tuckered out from the last one. I'll let one of the younger fellas take away that prize."

"Oh, but you must!" Her dark curls bounced adamantly. Then her eyes took on a different shine. "I'd love to see you win that one as well."

Glancing around at the number of people heading to the area of the three-legged-race, he reassessed Priscilla's plea. "Well, I might go over and watch—"

"Oh, splendid!" She grabbed his arm and trotted off in the direction of the next race with satisfied assurance.

Once at the starting line, he studied the entrants. Willy Albert, his own bunkhouse cook, was out there teamed up with Jake Turley, his ranch foreman. He gave the two men a wave and cheer of encouragement.

Several others, some known and others unfamiliar, were busy tying their legs together with the provided rope. A shout from the front arrested his attention. "Jonas!" It was Doc Foy, already paired up with none other than Mr. Bennet, the new shopkeeper. "Come on! Get on out here and join us!"

Caleb laughed. "Sorry, can't oblige. No partner."

At that moment Priscilla tugged on his sleeve. "I know where I can get you a partner!"

He looked at her skeptically.

"Honest!" she said, her eyes wide with a peculiar gleam. "I

know someone who just happens to be dying to be in the race, but is partnerless, too."

Visions of Priscilla's younger brother flashed through his mind. A tad on the scrawny side, but all-in-all a good kid. It might make him feel like part of the men if he participated. Caleb smiled indulgently. "Alright. Bring my partner on over. I'll go grab the ropes." He stepped forward as he watched Priscilla, almost giddy with glee, run off to fetch her brother. He took his place beside Jim Foy and Mr. Bennet. "Well, fellows. Looks like you've got your work cut out for you."

Noting both Mrs. Bennet and her elder daughter waiting along the sideline, he nodded at them in greeting.

"Good day, Mr. Jonas," John Bennet cordially greeted him. "Where's your partner?"

Caleb indicated with a nod behind him and squatted down to work on the jumble of ropes at his feet. "Priscilla's gone to fetch—"

A loud murmur of voices mixed with guffaws and gasps drowned him out. He pulled his attention away from the ropes he was trying to untangle and glanced up. He nearly toppled over in shock. There stood Miss Lydia Bennet, decked out in canvas trousers and a work shirt several sizes too large. Too busy glancing around her at the other contestants, she seemed not to notice him bent over.

Her initial look of confusion slowly faded and was replaced by one of sheer humiliation. Her delicate little face turned nearly as red as her fiery curls.

Caleb watched as her gaze darted from her father, then to her mother and sister standing on the sidelines, before finally settling on Caleb, who by now had stood up. As if the sight of him was the last straw, angry tears welled up in her almond-shaped emerald eyes. She turned and ran through the crowd of still chortling spectators—right past a highly amused Priscilla.

Under other circumstances, Caleb might have been tempted to laugh as well. But he sensed a different undercurrent here. He glanced at Lydia's father, who wore an expression of confusion combined with concern, and then to her mother, who appeared ten times more mortified than her daughter had.

One glance at the still giggling Miss Davis set the whole thing into perspective. Marching over to her and her entourage, Caleb dumped the mass of knotted rope at her feet. "This rope might be put to better use by tying up someone else."

"Oh, Caleb," she gushed, her merriment immune to his intense stare. "Don't tell me you didn't find that the least bit amusing."

Not bothering to answer her, he started off after Lydia.

❧

Lydia pushed her way through the tangle of branches and overgrowth, ignoring the stings of the ruthless foliage as it whipped at her face and tore at her hair.

How could she have been so stupid? So utterly gullible and foolish and naive.

She and her ridiculous competitiveness and pride. Hadn't her mother warned her it would be her undoing? Well, here she was. So thoroughly humiliated that at that moment she really wouldn't have cared had a wild animal pounced upon her and killed her. At least then she wouldn't have to face the consequences of her senseless actions.

She'd been so intent on winning a ridiculous race to try and one up that uppity Davis girl, knowing all the while there were other reasons—like attracting the attention of Mr. Caleb Jonas. Well, she cringed, she'd done that, hadn't she? A new wave of warmth enveloped her in shame.

Thoroughly exhausted by both her emotions and her tired muscles, she collapsed to the ground, heavy sobs wracking her whole being as those eternal seconds replayed themselves mercilessly. Then came the thoughts of what would happen next.

She'd been absolutely too abashed to so much as glance at her parents, but she knew. The words *St. Augustine's Ladies College* kept appearing in her mind. Only one solution remained.

Brushing the back of her scratched hand over her burning eyes, she stood and glanced around to get her bearings. She was already headed toward Laramie Peak, a fixed mark set upon the horizon. Pressing on more out of desperation than determination, she placed one foot in front of the other, hoping against hope that she'd reach that distant mountain before anyone found her.

❧

A firm grip on Caleb's arm halted him. He swivelled to find himself facing a seething Mrs. Bennet. "Just where do you think you're going?"

"Mrs. Bennet. I'm going to find your daughter."

"I think you are sorely mistaken!" Her blue eyes held a raging fire.

"Mary." Looking upset but not nearly as out of control, Mr. Bennet stepped up and took her arm from Caleb's.

"What?" she fairly exploded. "You want this man to go after our daughter after all that he's done?"

"I've done!" Caleb shot back. "Ma'am, I had nothing to do with—"

"I know." John Bennet's soft but firm voice interrupted them both. "I've been informed of the situation."

"Then you know I didn't have any idea—"

Mr. Bennet nodded his head. "But your going after her won't be necessary. I'll go."

Caleb let out an exasperated sigh. "Mr. Bennet, I know you want to find your daughter. But you've no knowledge of this area. I could cover much more—"

"Thank you, Mr. Jonas." His green eyes were kind yet determined. "But she's *my* daughter." With that, he escorted his wife away, her blazing look of wrath intensifying as she cast one final glance over her shoulder.

ten

Caleb watched helplessly from his position across the street, opposite the livery. Dusk was already beginning to settle across the lavender sky, and lantern-lit windows dotted the street. To the west, a large bank of heavy dark clouds threatened at the very least a good downpour.

Mr. Bennet's plan was utterly foolish—especially bordering on nightfall. But Caleb had seen him march into the stables with a determined set to his face. And now the store owner emerged, leading a young and obviously skittish filly. Squaring his shoulders, Caleb resolved to try once more.

Quickening his pace, he trotted up to the older gentleman. "Mr. Bennet," he started.

The man acknowledged him with a glance and a nod but did not alter his pace.

"I know. . ." Caleb struggled to find the appropriate words. "I can only imagine how you must feel, but please reconsider my offer."

They walked in silence for several seconds before John Bennet cleared his throat. "I thank you for your concern, Mr. Jonas." He finally slowed and, tugging gently on the horse's bridle, came to a stop. He looked Caleb squarely in the eyes, his steady gaze never wavering. "My daughter means the world to me. And I feel. . ." He paused as if trying to piece together exactly what to say. "I feel somewhat responsible for what happened today."

Caleb frowned in confusion. What on earth could her father have had to do with this fiasco?

A faint smile played across Bennet's lips. "I'm afraid some—no, *most*—of my daughter's stubbornness and mettle comes from me. And although at times it might lead her into new and pleasant experiences, it more often gets us both into a heap of trouble."

Caleb had to return a smile as thoughts of Lydia ambling onto the race course in trousers and tugging the oars of that small boat so aggressively came to mind.

"In any case," her father continued, "I need to find her and help her out of this. It's my duty."

Sighing in exasperation, Caleb tried once more. "At least let me accompany you. With the two of us we could—"

But John Bennet was already shaking his head. "I've incurred enough of my wife's wrath already. For some reason she has it fixed in her mind that you were in some way connected with this sordid set of circumstances."

Caleb opened his mouth to defend himself but was cut short.

"I know that is not the case. But in the end, it comes down to me, her father." His fixed look grew softer as he placed a hand on Caleb's shoulder. "I do thank you though, Mr. Jonas. Your offer is generous and proves you to be the type of man I thought you were." His lips turned up in an understanding smile. "Well, I'd best be off."

Watching the man mount and canter down the darkened street, Caleb felt a chill of foreboding travel through his bones. Where would he even begin to start looking? In this vast territory, how could one even know? And with this storm coming on. . .

Turning back toward the livery and his own horse, he stuffed his hands in his pockets. There his fingers met up with a small, slightly crumpled piece of paper. Snatching the note from its hiding place, he peered at the script on the now familiar missive. Darkness or not, he could have quoted the written words verbatim. This little piece of Lydia Bennet he carried with him—a little piece that perhaps only he knew.

That's when the thought struck. Wheeling around, he jogged in the direction of the mercantile. Rounding the rear corner of the two-story establishment, Caleb ducked quickly past the windows that looked as if they might house the parlor. He stopped and studied the myriad of panes above him. How would he ever discern. . . ?

A flicker of a shadow glided in front of a window, and Caleb dodged behind a stout cottonwood for cover. Peering cautiously at the lit windows, he waited. Eventually the occupant came into view. He watched as Sophia, combing out her long blond hair, paused to stand before the window. In the muted light from her lamp, her face revealed her obvious concern. For a few seconds he considered abandoning his plan. Did he want to add to the fear and worry Lydia's already troubled sister carried?

No, he argued with himself. *You're helping, remember?* Scanning the ground at his feet, he scooped up several of the tiniest pebbles he could find. Drawing in a breath, he pitched one gently at the glass. It met its mark with a gentle plink before falling back to the ground.

Sophia's brush stopped midstroke as she frowned into the night. Caleb stepped hesitantly from behind the tree and motioned with an upraised arm. Her eyes flared in surprise. Then she turned away from the window.

Muttering under his breath, he slumped back against the tree trunk. Great! Now what was he going to do? His initial plan wasn't working, and he didn't have any backup.

The click of a door latch sent him fully behind the tree's cover, flattening himself against it as he held his breath. Delicate footsteps shuffled down the wooden stairs, and he heard the crunch of the dried grass and dirt as whoever it was came nearer. He could only hope it was Sophia and not her mother.

The footfalls stopped just short of the tree, and he heard a quiet voice. "I believe Mother may be watching. I'm going down to the river. Once she sees where I'm headed, I'm confident she'll turn back to her business. You can follow then."

Without so much as a glance, Sophia walked calmly by his hiding place.

Caleb let out a shuddering breath, understanding that he needed to remain motionless for a few minutes more. They seemed longer than any he'd known.

He allowed an ample amount of time before cutting to his left and continuing until he was out of sight of the Bennet home. He'd head down the river farther over and cut back to meet Sophia.

It was slow going on this moonless night. When he finally reached the rippling, black water, he picked his way across the grassy embankment. Finally a short distance in front of him, he heard her voice over the chilly breeze that brought the scent of rain. "I'm over here."

He found his way, his eyes adjusting to the darkness surrounding her, and took a seat on the grass a respectful distance from her that would still allow them to speak quietly.

"Sorry to drag you out here at this time of night."

Uncomfortable silence prefaced her question. "What exactly do you want?"

"First off, I want you to know I had nothing to do with what happened today." He'd better get that squared away immediately. He'd no idea what her mother had told her.

"I know."

"Miss Bennet." He stopped and cleared his throat. This wasn't going to be as easy as he'd thought. As he played through his plan in his mind, he began to berate himself for a fool. But he was here, she was here, and senseless or not, he'd hauled her out here, so he'd best get on with it.

"I have something of your sister's," he started again. Gaining no response, he elaborated. "It's a note—well, not really a note. Not to me, anyway. But it's. . ." He blew out a long breath and dug in his pocket for the small paper. He handed it in her direction, and she took it somewhat hesitantly. It was then he realized that in the dark night it would be unreadable.

"It's a verse, a poem. I picked it up out of the river a few months back, when your family first moved here."

The young woman only stared.

"My point is, well—does she do that a lot? Write, I mean?"

"Yes, actually," came her perplexed answer. "Quite often."

"Do you think that I might be able to see some of her other

writings?" He saw her stiffen slightly and knew his intentions were far from clear. "I think they might help me find out where she might have gone. . .where she'll have headed."

"Does Daddy know about this?"

"No. Look, I know he wants to do this on his own, but I'm really concerned that he's in over his head here. He doesn't know this country. He doesn't know the surroundings, the places to avoid, the places to look, the dangers—"

"I agree."

"What?"

Her timid response was prefaced with a sigh. "I argued with him not to go. But he can be awfully stubborn. Even Dr. Foy wanted to accompany him, but Daddy said no. He had to do it himself."

The two sat in silence for several seconds, then Sophia turned to him.

"I know where she keeps her journal, but I'm not sure about handing it over. It's very personal to Lydia. Some of it she won't even show me."

Caleb swallowed hard. "I know. My father kept a journal. He was intensely private about many of his thoughts and ideas. But I also know that a lot of what he wrote revealed so much of who he was." Those bittersweet memories gathered in the stillness.

Pushing the thoughts from his mind, he went on. "It's not my desire to invade your sister's privacy, I assure you. But right now she's wandering around, completely unprotected and alone, in a thousand square miles of wilderness that she has no inkling about. I guess I'm willing to do whatever it takes to get her and your father back home as soon as possible."

"Why?"

Her question threw him, although he realized he should have expected it. Why, indeed? It would be easy to say it was just his duty. His calling left over from his previous occupation. To just show neighborly concern that nearly everyone tried to show in the territory. But even as he thought of the obvious explanation, other feelings struggled to reach the surface of his soul—ones that had been buried for no explicable reason other than confusion and fear. Why *was* it so important that he bring home that little redheaded waif safe and sound?

Grateful for the darkness that hid his flaming face, Caleb directed his response over the darkened waters of the North Platte. "It used to be my job."

Apparently the answer sufficed. Sophia was back on her feet, and he quickly followed suit. "I'll fetch the journal and place it on the back steps. You can retrieve it after I've been back inside long enough to distract my mother."

She started to walk back. After a few steps she stopped but did not turn to face him. "Please be careful, Mr. Jonas. I love my sister and father very much. I'm not sure how I would manage if I were to lose them." With that, she hastened her steps and disappeared in the darkness.

❧

Caleb finished throwing his gear into several packs, double-checking to see that he had enough extra food, clothes, and slickers for three people. He had debated leading another horse behind him, but the way the weather was shaping up, he opted against it. If this turned into the gully-washer that it promised, he'd have enough of a job keeping his own animal's footing steady.

Glancing around the livery's tack room, he was confident he'd remembered everything. There was only one more thing to do. He snatched up the bundle of papers he'd retrieved from the Bennet's back steps and sat on a nearby cot. He had to smile a few times as he noted the feminine sketches and drawings in some of the margins. But as he delved into the entries, he became engrossed. With each page a new facet of Lydia Bennet lay open, revealed to him. Several times he had to remind himself of the purpose for reading the pages. More than once he felt a twinge of guilt at reading someone's innermost thoughts.

He read over her accounts of coming to Veteran on the train, her detailed word pictures of new sights and landmarks, the wagon trip to Darby (reminding himself that within those entries was where she had written the piece he now carried). With the mention of encounters with Kid Cooley and Bradley Smyth, he felt an unaccountable surge of jealousy and also a bit of shame when he felt himself gloating over later entries where it was obvious she had no inclination toward either gentleman.

Conspicuously absent from her entries was any mention of him—not that he was expecting to be a subject of choice, but she'd covered several details of random encounters with other people. Yet his name was nowhere to be found. For some reason, that fact disturbed him.

When he finished the bulk of the pages, he let the papers slump to his lap. His mind was swirling with newfound knowledge of this young woman he had found so utterly intriguing from the moment he first saw her. He gave himself a mental shake. *Okay, Jonas. Think. From what you've got here, where do you suppose she'd go?*

Unconsciously shuffling around the papers, he straightened them into a stack. A wayward corner protruded stubbornly from one edge. Pulling out the errant sheet, he started to file it on top when he noticed it was folded in half. He curiously unfolded the wrinkled composition. It had been handled frequently.

Large bold letters blazed from the top of the page: *The Mountain's Son.* Another poem. He read on with burning curiosity.

If the moon came from the mountain tops
and illumined the rocky land
There'd be a man with a Stetson and a Winchester
who'd crossed many a sand.

Caleb balked before continuing. In spite of his discomfort in reading the other pages, he got the distinct feeling that he definitely shouldn't be reading this one. But he continued, not taking a breath until he'd read its conclusion. One portion had been scribbled out, and he tried in vain to decipher the lost words. Then he read it again.

Sitting back against the wall, he let out a deep breath. Would he dare be presumptuous enough to assume this referred to him? Yet a definite intuition told him it did. Folding the papers carefully, he stuffed them in one of the packs, and with renewed and intensified purpose, he jumped up from the cot, threw on his slicker, and went to ready his horse.

❧

John Bennet drew his hat farther down on his face for protection from the howling wind and stinging rain. It didn't relieve the situation. For the first time he began to realize that the rancher Jonas had been right. He was out of his element. If only this weather. . .

"Lydia!" he called out, only to have his voice swallowed by the intense gale. "Lydia!"

His poor filly, who'd been plodding along, suddenly stopped short. "Oh, come on," he coaxed as he urged her forward. "This is no time to quit on me!"

She stubbornly refused.

"Go on, I say!" But no amount of patting or prodding would move the beast, not even a swift kick to her sides. "Let's move, little lady. I need to find my Lydia!" he urged in desperation.

Just ahead of them a searing bolt of lightning pierced the darkness with such intensity it made John Bennet's eyes burn. An earsplitting crack of thunder followed almost immediately.

The nervous animal screamed a terrified whinny and reared up on her hind legs, sending her unprepared rider hurtling to the ground beneath.

"Lydia!" The cry scarcely escaped John Bennet's lips before his head collided with a sharp rock.

eleven

Caleb labored through the driving wind, its intensity magnified by the sting of the pelting rain. He pulled his slicker tighter about his neck and tipped his head to pour off some of the water that had collected on the brim of his hat.

Then common sense and experience brought him to a halt. This was utter madness. He couldn't see a foot in front of his face, and his new mount was growing more nervous with each flash of lightning and roar of thunder. The stallion had been broken, but this was too great a test. Even a seasoned animal would fight against these conditions. It was no use to continue.

He turned the drenched creature around, allowing the horse's natural instinct to lead him the few miles back toward town. But a feeling deep inside still battled with Caleb's decision to give up. He shuddered when he thought of all that could happen to a body out in these wilds—much less to a defenseless woman.

A faint sound caught Caleb's attention. Reining in his horse, he tried to discern the exact direction and source of the noise. It hadn't been a person, he was fairly sure of that. He noted the stallion had pricked his ears as well. "Good boy." He patted the wet neck. "Let's go see what that was, eh?"

He cautiously veered to the left and after a few steps heard it again. The low nicker of a horse.

He plodded onward, straining his eyes against the rain and darkness. At least the wind was at his back now. When the stallion stopped, he worried perhaps the animal was unsure of his footing. But another whinny indicated that the sought-after creature was directly in front of them.

Easing down from the saddle, he made sure to flip the reins over his mount's head, keeping a firm grasp on them just in case a jolt of lightning gave his mount any ideas of running off.

As he drew closer, he could finally make out the outline of the horse. It was the filly he'd seen Mr. Bennet leave town on, but John Bennet seemed to be nowhere near.

Leading the animal in a tight circle, Caleb noted no limps or any awkward gait, just the simple fright any beast acquires in such a tempest. Yet the horse's good condition was far from a relief. There was still the matter of her missing rider.

He led the animal to his own and tied a lead firmly from his saddle, then urged both horses forward. He refrained from calling out Mr. Bennet's name, partially because he knew it was useless to try and outscream the elements and also out of habit, training. One never gave away one's location so readily.

After about half a mile, the filly suddenly stopped, pulling slightly on her lead rope. He turned and looked at her. "What is it, girl?"

Again she strained on the tether, and he noted her preferred direction. Taking her lead, he urged his stallion to the southeast. They'd gone only fifty feet or so before both of them stopped. The filly lowered her head and blew out several breaths on the ground beside her. Frowning, Caleb grabbed his rifle, dismounted, and rounded in front of the pair.

When he nearly tripped over the body of a man, he recoiled. "Mr. Bennet!" Dropping to his knees, he carefully turned the man toward him. It was difficult to see in the blackness, but in cradling the older man's head, he felt the unmistakable warm stickiness of blood. Assuming the worst, he felt for a pulse. No, there was—wait. Yes! He detected a faint beat. Lunging for his saddlebag, he yanked out several cloths and wound a makeshift bandage around John Bennet's head.

Knowing that the outcome depended on his timeliness, he reached his arms around the wounded man and, as gently as possible, heaved him over the saddle of his own horse. He'd ride behind him. He couldn't take the chance of the filly rearing up again. Covering the man with one of his extra slickers,

Caleb settled himself into place and set out for town as fast as he dared.

By the time Caleb reached Darby, the squall had finally lightened to a steady downpour. The promise of dawn was held in the eastern sky. He rode in expecting to find a sleeping town, but to his amazement people were lining porches, storefronts, and boardwalks. His arrival brought an end to their vigil, and he began to realize just how tired he himself was.

Several men hurried toward him, and off to his side, a couple women ran toward the Bennets' residence. Doc Foy was the first to reach him. He stepped immediately to the saddle and, enlisting the help of Caleb and a couple other townsmen, gingerly removed John Bennet from his perch and carried him toward his home and office down the street.

One of the stable boys stepped forward and volunteered to care for the horses. Caleb nodded a thank-you as the lad walked past.

As Caleb helped carry the injured man, he discovered just how bad the wound was. The bits of cloth he'd placed in lieu of a bandage were soaked with blood, and he noted the man's ashen color. Catching Doc Foy's eye, he saw definite concern mingled with steely determination.

Reaching the two-story brick house, they ascended the front steps and wove through a lengthy hall, finally entering a room where they placed John Bennet on the bed.

"Thanks, fellows." Doc Foy nodded and indicated they could leave. He was obviously anxious to look over his patient.

Caleb started to close the door.

"Jonas." Doc's voice stopped him.

When he was beckoned in with a wave of the doctor's hand, he entered and shut the door behind him.

"Have any idea what happened?" Jim Foy asked without looking up from tending to his patient.

"Near as I can figure, his horse spooked and threw him. It was pretty dark out there. Hard to see exactly."

The doctor nodded as he began to unwind the bandages.

"And Lydia?"

Caleb fidgeted with the rim of his Stetson and slowly shook his head. "I'm going back out."

That brought a glance. "Caleb, why don't you let some of the other townsmen go? You've been out all night, and—"

"I'm going back out." He adjusted the damp hat on his head and turned to leave.

"Jonas."

He turned around once more.

Doc's expression softened with concern and understanding. "God go with you."

With a slight nod, he exited. Taking a deep breath, he leaned against the door jamb as he considered the man's parting words. He knew the doctor had meant well. But he'd also learned long ago to rely only on Caleb Jonas. Hadn't "God gone with" John Bennet and Caleb's own mother and father?

Halting any further thoughts along those lines, he stepped down the hall. He wanted to get shut of town before Mrs. Bennet arrived. He already knew her opinion of him and this . . .this he was sure would only add fuel to the fire.

Well, Doc better pray to that God of his that John Bennet would be fine—and that Caleb would find Lydia alive and in one piece.

❧

Lydia awoke to the sound of her teeth chattering. As she shivered uncontrollably, it took a few moments for her mind to sort out exactly where she was. Her sleep had been plagued with strange dreams and sounds, and as she assessed her surroundings she understood why.

Pushing herself up, she inched farther back under the outcropping of rock that left her just enough headroom to sit up. Her shirt sleeves and pant legs clung to her in icy dampness. That ledge hadn't offered much shelter in the wind.

It was growing lighter on the horizon, but the day wasn't dawning as clear as she'd hoped. Clouds still marred the skyline. She looked off in the direction of the mountains. There stood Laramie Peak, her intended destination, still appearing as far away as it had when she'd started yesterday.

But the distance no longer seemed so important. Her mind was finally beginning to think rationally. She was a fool. A complete fool. Here she sat—who knew how far away from anything—alone, cold, wet, and hungry in the unfamiliar barrenness of the plains.

The rock behind her poked unmercifully at her back and precluded any possibility of staying in a sitting position for too long. But she had other concerns. What would she eat? How would she ever get dry, warm?

Without a clue as to how to reach town, she realized the utter hopelessness of the situation. Hugging her stiff legs close to her, she leaned her head on her knees and wept. She'd never felt so close to death before. How much she'd taken for granted in what she'd deemed her dull life! Thoughts of home brought a fresh outburst of tears, knowing the panic she must be bringing her family. To relieve the ache, she did all she knew to do.

"Dear Lord," she whispered between shaky sobs. "What on earth have I gotten myself into? How many times have I been warned of my impetuousness? How many times have You, Yourself, convicted me of my stubborn pride?" She shook her head with thoughts of the previous day's incidents.

"Father, I humbly ask Your will. I know I've no right to ask for someone to find me. My own stupidity brought me here. Likely I'll have to find my way out of it. I pray You'll be with me, Lord. Give me the strength. Help me, Jesus. Help me." She cried until the exhaustion claimed her for another restless sleep.

❧

Bradley Smyth looked up from his desk as the young man stepped into his office. There was no pretense of courtesy in his gesture for the visitor to be seated. Both of them knew why they were here.

"So." His guest's tone suggested cocky bravado as he leaned back easily in his chair. Smyth eyed him critically, trying to discern if that was an asset for this particular situation or not. "What's up, Mr. Banker?" Two boot heels, none too clean, found their way to the edge of the mahogany desk.

Smyth shot him a look that needed no reinforcement. The boots were removed. Bradley decided to ignore the incident and get straight to the point.

"How is Bennet faring?"

A shrug. "No one's real sure. Doc won't let anybody but the Missus and his daughter in there."

The banker nodded as he rubbed his temples. "Okay, then. Tell me, what do you know of Caleb Jonas?"

The face before him showed no surprise at the question. Steely gray eyes glinted for a moment before a response came. "Been doing some checking into that. Other than the obvious stuff, his ranch, his hired hands, etc., it's hard to pinpoint anything on the guy. It's like up until three years ago when he moved here, he never existed."

Smyth smirked. "He's not as elusive as he would seem. You just need to know the right people."

The fellow leaned forward and in a quiet voice said, "You know, I did hear that he was a Texas Ranger."

"Blast!" Smyth's hand came down hard on the desk, causing the young man to jump. "You don't think I already know that? What is this fascination and fear of the rangers? So he went around toting a pistol for a few years, taking potshots at cattle thieves. Big deal!"

No response.

Bradley raked his fingers through his hair. "Look, I don't care about his past. I'm looking at now. I just want to know how much I can count on you should I deem you worth hiring."

A suspicious glance shot across the desk. "What are you wanting me to do exactly? Kill the guy? It's not like I can walk up to him in broad daylight and—"

"Of course not, you simpleton. I just want him. . .out of the picture for a while. Distracted." He smiled briefly. "Detained."

"Why? I don't get it."

Smyth impatiently shuffled some papers together. "That's

really not your concern, is it? As long as you get paid, you'll do as I say."

"Hey, I don't take orders from nobody." He straightened in his chair and thrust out his chest.

With a disparaging glance, the banker stood from the desk. "Then find yourself work elsewhere." He turned and busied himself, sorting through a stack of files on a cabinet behind him. He knew the boy was trying to sort through it all with what little intelligence he had. Why did he always end up having to deal with these imbeciles?

"Okay, okay. Whaddya want me to do?"

Smyth turned and gave him an indulgent smile. "Well, now. That's more like it." He reseated himself and clasped his hands together. "I'm only going to go through this once. Understood?"

A nod.

"Good. And one other thing. If you're ever asked, you were never in here today, or any other day for that matter. Clear?"

"Yeah, yeah. Just let me have my chance back at him. What do I need to do?"

"The first thing you need to do is make yourself acquainted with the Bennet family. Clean yourself up, look presentable, use some manners if you have any. Become that nice young man who works hard on area ranches."

This was met by an amused grin. "A regular Jack-dandy, eh?"

"Exactly. Oh, what's your given name?"

A flush fell across already ruddy cheeks. "Bertram" was mumbled in the direction of the floor.

"Fine. From now on you're Bertram. Bertram Cooley."

Smyth felt the corners of his lips curl up as the next phase of his plan fell into place.

twelve

The sun finished its game of hide-and-seek with the horizon and began its upward climb, its blazing glow promising a hot day. Caleb lowered the rim of his Stetson to avoid the most direct rays. At least it wasn't raining. But taking a quick survey of the ground, he realized the favorable conditions didn't mean a whole lot. Any tracks had been completely wiped away by the gully-washer of the night before.

Undaunted, he pressed on, urging the older dun gelding ahead. The stallion he'd ridden yesterday had remained slightly skittish after he'd returned to town, so Caleb had stopped to swap with his oldest, most dependable horse. The one, in fact, who'd been with him during his last years in Texas and had carried him home to Darby. If any creature was accustomed to searching the wilds for missing persons, it was this one.

Scanning the surrounding landscape, he squinted against the brightness, trying to discern any out-of-place objects among the clumps of sagebrush, grasses, and occasional tumbleweed.

It was nearly noon before Caleb stopped. Taking a swig of water from his canteen, he allowed his horse to steal a few sips from a small trickling creek. The sun blazed down unmercifully on man and beast. Kneeling beside the creek, Caleb removed his hat and splashed the refreshing water over his face and neck.

Rising to his feet, a sound met his ears. He stilled and listened for it again. Several minutes ticked by. Nothing.

He remounted the dun and started over a small knoll to the west. At the top of the hill, he saw her. There below, still garbed in her baggy trousers and torn and smudged shirt, Lydia trudged ahead, every so often her unsteady gait causing her to weave to one side or the other.

A burst of renewed energy washed through him just at the sight of her, alive. Suddenly she stumbled. He spurred his horse before her arms tried to catch her fall forward.

Reining in and dismounting at her side, he expected a terrified reaction to his sudden appearance, but she merely pulled her head up from her arms, looked him squarely in the eye, and, after the hint of a tired smile, began to cry.

For the first time in his life, Caleb stood frozen, with no idea what to do. Emotions tumbled around inside of him: outright relief that she was alive, fear that she was hurt or injured, apprehension about what she had encountered or endured since yesterday, and a myriad of other feelings he couldn't identify.

Her delicate features were reddened, not just from weeping, but from a severe sunburn. Her coppery curls were in a mass of knots and frizz, and her watery green eyes looked so pitiful as she gazed at him imploringly. He'd never seen a more welcome or appealing sight. A hard lump formed in his throat, and with all his might, he fought the urge to grab her into his arms.

A mental shake reset the scene, and duty and training reclaimed their positions. Dropping to his knees, he helped her to a sitting position and offered her a drink from his canteen. As she greedily drank the long-needed water, Caleb took the opportunity to ascertain if any of her limbs had succumbed to breaks or sprains. Everything seemed sound. Leaning back on his heels, he studied her carefully. Other than the obvious sunburn and slight dehydration, she appeared to be fine. He was astounded. It was inconceivable that she'd not been injured or been harmed by snakes or any number of other dangerous animals.

His eyes met her face again and found her staring at him with intense pleading in her eyes. It made him uncomfortable. Then he realized he hadn't spoken to her yet. Clearing his throat, he glanced at the ground before meeting her fixed look once more. "You alright?"

She hesitated a second before nodding.

Plucking his hat from his head, he reached over and placed it gently on her tangled ringlets. The rim was huge and slipped down precariously, nearly covering her eyes. She pushed the brim up slightly and looked out from under its shadow. Once again, Caleb was overtaken with a yearning to grab this slip of a girl and protect her with all he possessed.

But he did have to choke back a chuckle at the oversized hat. "It'll keep you from getting too much more sun," he explained. Then he scooped her effortlessly off the ground, wondering if the waif weighed a hundred pounds dripping wet. Thoughts of what it might feel like to hold her in an unofficial capacity flitted across his mind, causing him to frown in concentration and try to keep focused on his task.

It was then he noticed her feet, still clad in her dainty little button-up boots, albeit a heel missing from one of them and a host of tears and scratches marring the once-white leather. He shook his head, wondering how she could have made it as far as she did in those ridiculous shoes. Placing her tenderly on his horse, glad for the trousers she still wore, he stuck his boot in the stirrup and swung up behind her.

He adjusted the reins and repositioned himself so she would be comfortable. "Shall we get you home?"

She nodded, still not having said anything.

The gelding plodded on as if knowing that a five- or six-hour ride stretched in front of them. In less than five minutes, Caleb noted the increasing heaviness of Lydia's nods. With every bob of her head, she slowly leaned back, finally succumbing to the long-awaited sleep, her head falling back against his shoulder. Caleb drew in a long breath as he fought to banish a barrage of unbidden thoughts.

Do something productive, Jonas. Remember, your job is just to get her home. He readjusted the Stetson so that it would better shield her from the sun and provide a bit of darkness for her to doze in.

As they rode on, he couldn't resist basking in the enjoyment of his renewed role of protector and guardian, and he didn't stop to wonder why he worked so hard to convince himself that these feelings were merely the echoes of his assignments years ago.

❧

Strange thoughts and images fluttered in and out of Lydia's mind, swirled in a fog of haziness. Voices and events mingled in a cacophony of confusion. One minute she was at the store, stocking shelves and bantering with her father, the next she was standing humiliated in front of a crowd of jeering onlookers.

Gradually the images faded away, and she was aware only of the rhythmic plod of horse's hooves and the gentle sway of the animal's easy gait. Opening her eyes, she saw pitch darkness. Startled, she sat up too abruptly and sent a hat falling into her hands. It all came back to her. Once again she battled her desires to cry out with indignity or let flow tears of relief.

She ventured a look back at her benefactor. His dark brown eyes greeted her kindly as his full lips tweaked at one corner to give her a lopsided smile. His eyes returned to the trail, and she stole a few more seconds to study this hero who had saved her. Or rather whom the Lord had sent. She remembered her earlier prayer, and she breathed up a new one of grateful thanks.

Upon raising her lids from the brief petition, her gaze happened to fall near Caleb's neckline. There, peeking above his collar, was that familiar scar. A flush of embarrassment crept over her as she turned her face away, ashamed of studying him so intimately.

From her back, she felt the slow rumble of laughter buried deep in his chest. She cast a wary eye to her side, wondering if she again was the source of his amusement, and she felt her color heighten.

He finally broke the silence. "You're dying to know, aren't you?"

"Whatever do you mean?"

Ignoring her attempt at feigning ignorance, he continued. "I'll tell you if you'll keep it to yourself. It's not something I'm particularly proud of."

Lydia nodded, too engrossed in the prospect of hearing the story behind the wicked-looking scar to remember she'd been playing dumb.

"I was about eighteen. A wild fool. Working on a ranch down in Texas. Thought I was one of the big boys, whooping and hollering and drinking to keep up with the rest of them." He shook his head at the recollection.

"A group of us headed to town one night and hit the saloon pretty hard. Thought I was in a fine condition to ride right on back to the bunkhouse, so I tore down the main street and down several side streets as fast as I could. It was a big deal to show off a horse's speed.

"Well, mine was a quick one alright. Quicker than my addled brain, unfortunately. He headed me right through someone's yard, which was strung neatly with several strands of wire for a clothesline."

Lydia gasped as she pictured the scene.

Caleb laughed again. "Fool kid! The doc was right; I deserved to lose my head after that stunt. But here I am. Not too much worse for wear—other than I probably won't be winning any oratory contests anytime soon."

Frowning in thought, she concentrated on his raspy voice. It wasn't severely impaired, but it sounded distinct. She'd had no idea what could cause something like that. Suddenly she laughed. She'd heard some of the rumors in town about that scar: Indian fights, murderous desperadoes holding him at knifepoint. . .

"Let's keep it a secret, huh?" Caleb asked.

She agreed, her giggles fading away. "So what else did you do in Texas besides work on a ranch?" she asked. She was determined to make the most of their time by unraveling some of the mysteries surrounding this man.

"Well, I was a ranch hand for three years. Then in '72, I joined up with the Texas Rangers. They'd been out of commission for a while after the war. Had a group of shady characters in there who called themselves the state police. A little too political for many people's liking. So the rangers were brought back. I served with them five years. Then I came back here."

Lydia turned and studied him, easily picturing him in that role. He looked a trifle uncomfortable under her scrutiny and she turned away again. "A Texas Ranger. . .what was it like?"

He paused. "They were a good group of men," he finally said. "The best. The unit I was in was called the special force. Captain McNelly led it. Best military man I've ever known."

"McNelly?" Lydia remarked. "I remember hearing that name. Wasn't his the first group to ever bring back stolen cattle from across the Mexican border?"

Caleb grinned with a bit of pride. "Yeah, that was us. Thirty of us against a band of several hundred Mexicans."

She stared in wide-eyed wonder. "What an incredible life. I can't believe all that you've done. . .all that you've been through."

Caleb was unaccountably quiet for some time. Lydia didn't understand his sudden reserve until she noted the dark circles under his eyes and the tight look to his face. Then she felt guilty, knowing she was the cause of his lack of sleep. There was no way she could frame an apology that would cover all her imprudent actions, so she took shelter in the silence as well.

❧

They were still several hours from Darby when Caleb decided to stop for a rest. The last hour had been ridden in silence—uncomfortable, yet a blessing. Plaguing his thoughts was the problem of how to broach the subject of her father. How much should he tell her? Should he say anything at all? He'd have to think on that one.

Then there was the question of her enamored view of his life. How much of that should he correct? Not that anything he'd said had been a lie. But where did a person temper the glories with the heinous scenes of watching a friend and fellow ranger get shot off his horse, or toting off another destined to die of a fatal wound. Or the sickening recollection of digging through the stubbled and burned-out remains of his own family's home, knowing he'd never see his parents or brother again.

They'd settled next to a grassy knoll to eat a bite before continuing the rest of the way to Darby. As they chewed on the biscuits and jerky, Lydia gradually settled back into conversation. "I. . .prayed and prayed for someone to find me," she confessed at last. "I'm just so relieved that the Lord sent you when He did. But then, I suppose you must have had heaps of experience tracking people down."

Ignoring her references to God, Caleb tried his best to respond to her chatter politely. He was still wrestling with feelings and quandaries that he didn't know how to place. Like why every time he watched her talk or laugh or go through some little mannerism, he felt like he wanted to be nowhere else. This sensation. . .this was a new one to him, and very unsettling.

"I'm thirsty," Lydia piped up suddenly. "Would you like some water, too?" She jumped up from her spot on the grass and headed for his horse.

She'd already begun to rummage through several of his saddlebags when he bolted to his feet. "Wait. I'll get it—"

"No, I'll find it. I know I saw you put it somewhere in. . ."

Caleb stopped short when he heard her shuffling through a raft of papers.

"Hmm, what's this?"

Caleb hunkered down and raked his fingers through his hair. Without raising his head, he let his eyes wander in her direction. She appeared from behind the horse, holding the stack of papers. Her face was ashen, her eyes blazing, and her hands shaking. It was a moment before she could even speak. "What—what is. . .where did you get this?"

Caleb took a deep breath as he stood and slowly approached her. "I got it. I needed it to help find you." That sounded lame even to him.

Her emerald eyes flashed dangerously. "You read this? You actually read my personal journal?"

He nodded.

Lydia shook her head incredulously. "My journal. My private thoughts, my ideas, my poems." She shot him a horrified glance. "All of it?" she whispered.

This time Caleb shuffled his feet before forcing himself to look directly at her. "Yes."

The anger on her face burned away and was quickly replaced by a look of hurt and humiliation ten times greater than what she'd worn at the picnic.

He reclaimed the papers from her unresisting hand and stuffed them carefully back in the saddlebag. Making himself busy preparing the horse for departure, he watched as her eyes misted over and her look moved a million miles away.

He could have kicked himself for suggesting such a thing to her sister in the first place. Had he really *needed* the journal? Or was it the intense curiosity he'd felt ever since reading her note at the river?

Not that the answers to these questions would make any difference. The lady's look said everything he needed to know about how she felt about him.

Avoiding her eyes, he stated, "We'd better get going."

Woodenly she allowed him to assist her up. He followed suit, painfully aware of the distance between them. . .a chasm he wasn't sure could ever be crossed.

thirteen

Just past sundown, Caleb and Lydia rode into the dusk-lit main street of Darby. Lydia glanced around the area buildings. Everything seemed quieter than usual for early evening. In a sense she was relieved. It would save her the horror of having to face all the people who watched her run in the first place.

Caleb turned at the Bennets' and took her directly to the back door. After dismounting, he reached up for her and lifted her to the ground. She stiffened under his touch. All the way home the lines of that poem she'd written kept running through her mind. He'd certainly read that one as well. Of all the. . .

Well, she'd confront Sophia as soon as she was able. Her sister was the only one who knew where the journal was kept—or that it even existed.

Caleb had swung back into the saddle. A prick at her conscience made Lydia set aside her feelings. This man had saved her life. At the very least, she owed him a sincere thank-you. She'd never be able to repay him for all he'd done.

Yet the rest of the feelings, the ones she'd expressed in the journal, were still there as well, much to her frustration. But she was determined to rise above it all. She'd express her gratitude and be done with the matter. Lifting her chin, she raised her lashes and gazed up at the towering rancher. Something in his expression made her forget all she was going to say.

For a timeless moment his eyes held hers. Then he slid down from his saddle and dug into the saddlebag, withdrawing the papers that had caused such pain. He held them out tentatively. "I. . .I'm very sorry. I'd no right to these."

Lydia accepted them without comment, cradling them in her arms. She knew she'd better have her say before she lost her nerve completely.

"Thank you, Mr. Jonas. I know I caused my parents no end of grief over my actions, and I'm extremely grateful that you were willing to come and search for me." There. It was out.

His face held a trace of confusion, but he only muttered a hushed "You're welcome."

Caleb suddenly stepped forward and took hold of her arms, his deep eyes searching her own. "Lydia," he whispered. "I—"

The door behind them squeaked open.

"Lydia?" came a timid voice.

Caleb immediately loosened his grasp, but the warmth of his touch lingered. Nor could she dismiss the troubled look on his brow.

She turned and was immediately enveloped by her sister's slim arms. Lydia returned the embrace. "I'm okay, Sophia," she assured her softly. "Everything's okay."

But the older girl clutched her all the more tightly as a sob shook her tiny frame.

Lydia eased her away to arms' length. Sophia's eyes were swollen and her face blotchy as if she'd been crying a long, long time. Fear skittered up Lydia's spine.

Caleb stepped forward. "Miss Bennet," he began hesitantly, and Lydia glanced at him, noting the intense concern on his face. "Is everything—"

The fragile hold Sophia had on her composure crumbled as she shook her head, a fresh whimper causing her to gasp in little breaths. "Lydia," she finally managed to whisper as her blue eyes welled up and sent tears coursing down her pale cheeks. "It's Daddy. He's. . .he's. . ."

Caleb was at Sophia's side in an instant, supporting her arm. "I think we'd best go in and sit down in the house."

Lydia, however, remained rooted in place as she glanced from one to the other. Something was going on here that only she was unaware of.

She grabbed Caleb's sleeve, effectively halting him. "No.

Sophia, tell me *now* what has happened."

Her sister gazed at her unwaveringly. "Our daddy. . .is dead." A sob nearly broke off Sophia's last word as she buried her face in her hands.

Lydia felt her own heart thud to a stop. She stared at her sister in confusion. What on earth was she talking about? What could have happened to their father?

She studied her weeping sister, then looked at Caleb. "Daddy—" She couldn't even utter the last words.

Sophia only nodded shakily.

As the dreaded reality began to sink in, Lydia's head reeled. "Oh, Daddy," she whispered. Blackness fell over her like a smothering blanket.

❧

Caleb removed his hat and ran his fingers through his hair before entering the white clapboard building. Stepping through the door, he hung his Stetson on one of the empty hooks, straightened his string tie, and rounded the partial wall dividing the entry from the front room.

The building certainly looked different than it had on the occasional Saturday night when Caleb had attended the town social and dance. The atmosphere was far different as well.

His gaze shifted uncomfortably as he felt several pairs of eyes noting his entrance. The small schoolroom was filled to near bursting with people. There didn't seem to be a chair left to be had. He caught Doc Foy's nod from the opposite side and worked his way through the somber throng to join his friend.

A cordial handshake greeted Caleb as Jim Foy made room where he stood against the wall, the only place left to occupy.

Caleb scanned the room. Everyone from the surrounding area seemed to have come. In the front of the room, a newly made pine box rested upon two sawhorses. Caleb swallowed hard and shifted his attention elsewhere. He still couldn't believe that Mr. Bennet. . . He hadn't known Lydia's father *well,* but the man seemed a friendly sort. He'd reminded Caleb a bit of his own father.

Caleb turned his focus to the front bench. The three Bennet women sat stoically, dressed in the customary black. He couldn't see their faces, but as he studied them, a curly red head turned. He watched her look around the room, observing her drawn face and the listlessness to her normally sparkling eyes. The sight brought an ache to his heart. He shot a glance down to his boots before lifting his head again. She'd found him. Her eyes penetrated him, and he felt vulnerable and exposed.

This poor girl. Not only had he shattered her confidence in him—and likely any man at this point—but he felt a trace of responsibility for her father's death. Maybe if he'd found Mr. Bennet sooner, maybe if he'd been more attentive to the man's wounds, if he'd gotten him to Darby faster. . .

The doubts had plagued his mind constantly since hearing of her father's death. All he could do now was cowardly avoid her glance, suddenly and painfully aware that the strength of Caleb Jonas on which he'd depended for the last ten years was completely inadequate.

The preacher stepped to the front of the room, and Caleb shifted his weight and sighed, memories from far too many similar scenes filling his thoughts.

Following the simple service and brief internment in the little cemetery on the town's outskirts, Caleb drifted back with the majority of the hushed crowd. A few people ventured to speak in normal tones. In a territory, life went on no matter how cruel the break to family and friends. How well Caleb knew.

Having buried his own family years ago, he didn't care to count the number of times he'd been sent along with the captain to the homes of wives and parents with the tragic news of some young man's untimely death in the rangers.

Caleb caught sight of Lydia walking arm in arm with her sister. Near her other side, Smyth hovered protectively. A twinge shot through Caleb as he watched the man's demeanor. There was something about that man that rankled him, and he wasn't about to chalk it up to plain old jealousy in spite of the fact that he painfully wanted to be near Lydia himself. He'd thought it best to let her take the initiative. She deserved at least that much respect after all she'd endured.

Jim Foy fell into step beside him. "How are you doing, Jonas?"

Caleb shrugged. "Okay, I guess. How are *they* doing?" He nodded in the direction of the three women.

Foy stared ahead, frowning as he studied the ladies. "Fair." He shoved his hands in his pockets. "You know, it's kind of surprised me, but Sophia has been dealing with this the best of any of them. She's a lot stronger than she appears. Mrs. Bennet isn't saying a whole lot. It's her way, I believe. She's concentrating on what's best for the girls right now."

Caleb waited for Jim's assessment of Lydia, but none came. When he glanced up at his friend, he noticed him watching something ahead of them. Following Foy's gaze, Caleb stared in uncomfortable silence.

Mary Bennet led her two daughters straight toward Caleb and his friend. "Gentlemen."

"Mrs. Bennet." Jim spoke first. "Let me express again my deep regret and sympathies for you and your daughters. I'm truly sorry."

The widow's eyes watered for a fraction of a second before she squared her shoulders. "I know. And I thank you for all you've done, Dr. Foy. I know John thought very highly of you, and you've proven yourself in our eyes as well."

She peered up at Caleb, who just remembered to remove his hat. "Mr. Jonas. If it wouldn't be an inconvenience to you, I was wondering if you'd be free to stop by our residence this evening. There is something of importance I'd like to discuss with you."

Caleb stood unnerved. He'd never imagined being invited to the Bennets' home for any reason. Flicking a glance toward Lydia, he tried to read some clue from her face, but she seemed just as surprised as he was. He nodded. "Of course. I'll stop by after the supper hour, if that's convenient."

When it had all been agreed upon, Mary Bennet turned, and Dr. Foy joined in escorting them home. Lydia remained behind for a stolen second. "I just wanted to thank you again," she said in a hushed voice. She seemed in a hurry to get out what she wanted to say. "And I'm sorry. . .for being angry with you." Her gaze fell to the ground briefly before returning to his face. "Sophia explained everything to me."

"Lydia," he returned, only half aware that he'd just used her first name in addressing her. "You have every right to be angry with me. I violated your privacy, your trust."

She shook her head and smiled sadly. "You saved my life, Mr. Jonas. For that, I can never repay you."

She was doing it again. Looking up at him with those glimmering eyes, making him forget everything about who and where he was. He reached for her hand, his gaze never leaving hers. "Lydia, do you have any idea what your mother—"

"Lydia!" Mrs. Bennet's voice broke the reverie. "We need to get home."

Caleb dropped Lydia's hand, aware that not only Mrs. Bennet, but likely half the town had seen that little episode. Well, not much he could do about it now.

Before she turned, Lydia shook her head no. But she mouthed the word *later* before rejoining her party. Once again, Caleb observed, it included Bradley Smyth.

❧

Quarter past seven. Caleb stuffed his timepiece back into his pocket and drew in a deep breath before knocking on the rear door of the Bennet home.

It didn't take long for Mrs. Bennet to answer the door. She greeted him with a polite, if somewhat stilted, smile. "Come in, Mr. Jonas." He doffed his hat, ducked in the door, and followed her as she retreated to the sitting room.

The house was unaccountably quiet. He saw no trace of Lydia or Sophia. Perhaps they were waiting in the parlor. But that room was empty as well. A sinking feeling began to grow within him.

"Please." She indicated a chair. "Be seated."

Caleb sat rigidly on the delicate seat, toying idly with the hat still in his hands while Mrs. Bennet took her place across from him.

Neither spoke, and Caleb found the silence unnerving. Finally Mrs. Bennet opened the conversation. "Mr. Jonas, you must know we owe you a great debt for finding our Lydia." She hesitated momentarily. "And for John, as well."

Caleb nodded. "I wish I could have done more."

"Of course." She studied him for an uncomfortable length of time.

"Where *is* Lydia this evening?" Caleb asked.

"She's out tonight. Taking a ride with Mr. Smyth." Again she seemed to wait for his reaction.

"I see. It's nice she is able to get out for a time after all that's happened."

"I quite agree." Mary Bennet paused. "Mr. Jonas, what exactly are your intentions toward my daughter?"

He shuffled his feet in apprehension. Hadn't he asked that very same query of himself a thousand times in the last several days? Months? He was tired of tiptoeing around the subject. The woman was right. It was time to get this out in the open and be forthright about the whole matter.

"Mrs. Bennet," he faced her with new resolve. "I think your daughter is the most interesting, charming woman I've ever met."

Her composed face registered no surprise. After a minute, she stood and paced the room a few times. "Mr. Jonas." She turned toward him, her look penetrating. "I've long been aware of your feelings for my daughter. Now that you've confirmed them, I must ask of you just one thing."

Caleb gave a nod of assent.

"Stay away from her."

"What?" Caleb was on his feet before the word escaped his lips.

"I will make this brief, as Lydia is expected back any moment." She clasped her hands together, resting her thumbs against her lips before she began. "Lydia and her father are. . . *were* alike in many ways. They both harbored this. . .this *wanderlust* for ridiculous adventure, new experiences." She rolled her eyes at the recollection.

"My point is this," she went on. "Lydia's foolish temper caused her to run off, and John's foolish pride caused him to run after her. Neither of them gave the slightest consideration to what might lie ahead."

Caleb listened, still numb. Where was she heading with this?

"My daughter needs someone solid, stable, dependable. One who'll keep her out of trouble."

Caleb swallowed a breath of frustration. "Mrs. Bennet, I understand your concern. But Lydia's not a child. She's fully capable of making her own decisions. Part of maturing is learning from past mistakes. Heaven knows, I've learned a lot from mine."

"Exactly. Don't you see? You're precisely what Lydia *doesn't* need."

"Pardon me?" Anger began to rise in Caleb's chest.

"Mr. Jonas," her condescending voice continued, "I have no doubt that you are an excellent rancher and a good person. But you appear to me to be too much of what wouldn't be in my daughter's best interest. John nurtured in her this obsession for wild experiences, and look where it got them."

Caleb stood astounded at her assumptions. "Are you implying that this was *my* fault?"

"No. I'm saying this is who Lydia is. This is how she reacts to things. And the last thing she needs is someone with similar tendencies."

Caleb had tried his hardest to be polite, but the longer Mrs. Bennet talked, the more his back stiffened. With as calm a voice as he could muster, he replied, "Ma'am, you don't know me from Adam, if you'll pardon my frankness. Where on earth do you get the idea that I'm yearning for wild experiences?"

Her face showed the slightest trace of embarrassment. "Well," she foundered. "I've heard from sources about your—"

"From *whom?"* he pressed.

"From. . .those about town and—"

His snort of derision cut her off. "So, you're willing to rely on gossip about the integrity of a man's character?"

She blanched. "I don't think that—"

"Mrs. Bennet," he countered again. "Let me tell you something. When you've lived in as many small towns as I have, you learn something. Never, and I mean *never* believe everything you hear. Had I fallen under the assumption that everything I heard about *you* is true, I'd never have come here tonight."

Her blue eyes widened as she stared at him half in horror, half in indignation. "Whatever do you mean?"

"Well, who knows what would have been said about me after I left the house of a notorious gossip." He grabbed his hat from the nearby chair. "Good night, ma'am."

Without so much as a glance in her direction, he stalked through the door and out of the Bennet house for the first and *last* time.

fourteen

Without Father's lively presence, the breakfast table seemed oppressively quiet at the Bennet house. Lydia wondered if the emptiness would ever go away or if she would just have to learn to live with it. She spread a thin layer of jam across her muffin while she watched Sophia sit dejectedly, her food untouched, her eyes still rimmed with red.

A glance at her mother showed the woman still engrossed in perusing a newspaper. Her demeanor since Father's death hadn't changed noticeably other than that she didn't seem as apt to pounce on Lydia. For the most part, she was quiet, reflective.

Much of the morning's heaviness, Lydia knew, had to stem from whatever had transpired last evening. She'd been anticipating the arrival of Caleb, but to her chagrin, she had opened the door to find an exceedingly gracious Bradley Smyth. He'd come to take her for a ride, and her mother had all but pushed her out the door. Seeing no way out, Lydia had agreed, hoping that she and the banker would return before Jonas left.

No such luck. She'd arrived home to a silent house. Her mother had apparently settled in for the night, and a morose Sophia stared vacantly out her window. No amount of coaxing had revealed what was the matter with her sister.

Now they sat silently at breakfast. Lydia's mother finally laid aside her paper and looked pointedly at her daughters. "I'm off to make a few visits about town. The mercantile will not be open today. In fact, the store won't be opening again, save for any emergency items people may need."

Lydia started. "What?"

Her mother returned a condescending stare. "What did you expect, Lydia? That we'd manage the thing ourselves?"

Lydia sat in shocked silence.

"Sophia." Her mother had turned her attention to her older daughter. "You know what needs to be done. I'd like you to start your packing. You may fill Lydia in on the plans so she knows what to pack as well."

Before Lydia could protest, her mother was out the door, pinning her hat to her head as she went.

Sophia idly pushed her plate away as she rose and solemnly turned toward the stairs. Lydia sat for a few mute seconds, trying to determine if she were having a bad dream. But each thud of Sophia's ascending footfalls made her very aware of the reality of it all. Jumping up from her chair, she chased up the steps, reaching the top just as her sister grabbed a large valise from the hall.

Yanking the handle from Sophia's unresisting grip, Lydia stared at her. "Tell me. Tell me now. What is going on?"

Her sister's face registered pathetic resignation. "We're leaving." She reclaimed the luggage and headed for their bedroom. "The day after tomorrow. We need to pack."

Lydia watched her sibling's retreating back in utter amazement. "Sophia!" she nearly screamed, succeeding in stopping her sister in her tracks. "What are you doing? You're just going to let her. . .you're not even going to. . ."

Lydia stopped, took a breath, and continued in a quieter voice. "What about Dr. Foy?"

The mention of his name seemed to break the thread that held Sophia's resolve. Her pale blue eyes clouded, then welled up with tears. Tiny sobs began to shake her thin shoulders.

Lydia immediately ran to her, embracing the girl. "I'm sorry. I didn't mean to make you upset."

Sophia shook her head helplessly. "It's not you. It's just—" She broke off as another sob claimed her voice.

Lydia escorted her into their room, sat them both on her bed, and cradled Sophia tenderly until the crying lessened.

"Sophia?" she queried softly, handing her a hankie from her own pocket. "Can you please just tell me what has happened?"

Dabbing at her eyes, Sophia sniffled. "It's just that. . .with

Daddy gone, Mother doesn't think we could make it very well here. And you know she never really wanted to come to Darby anyway—"

"Sophia," Lydia interrupted. "I know all that. Tell me what's going on with you." Lydia tapped effectively on her sister's forehead. "In here. And in your heart."

When she was met by Sophia's troubled gaze, she ventured on. "Really, Soph. I'm your sister, remember? I know. I can see. You've been so. . .so listless for months. Even before we moved to Darby. What happened?"

A deep sigh preceded Sophia's reply. "It's always going to be the same, Lydia. Always." Rising up from her place on the bed, Sophia crossed the room and stared out the far window. "I half envied you when you ran away. Did you know that? I almost wished that I had that kind of courage, fortitude."

"I think stupidity is the word you're searching for," Lydia scoffed. "That had to be the most foolish thing I've ever done."

Sophia turned back to her. "But you did *something*. That's my point. Me?" She shook her head in disgust. "I just stay and take it." Toying idly with the hankie, she continued. "What you may not have known is that a young man was interested in calling on me back in Independence."

Lydia stared openly. "Who?"

"Zachary."

"Zach?" she asked incredulously. "Zach Peters?" She'd had no idea that there'd even been anything more than polite contact between her sister and the young man who'd been apprenticing under her father as a shopkeeper. She frowned as she remembered the meek young man. He'd been so quiet that Lydia had scarcely been aware that he was around. But then, he was a lot like Sophia in that way.

Sophia nodded. For the first time Lydia put it all together. Her sister's sad demeanor, the move to Darby, everything. No doubt her mother, as much as she hated the thought of moving to a small town like Darby, was relieved that it would save her daughter from marrying a mere shopkeeper. The thought made Lydia's blood boil.

But more than that was the intense shame and regret she felt. True, she hadn't known any of this, but her conscience railed that she *should* have. This was her sister, after all. And she was too wrapped up in her foolish, immature dreams to see that her sister was hurting. She began to cry.

"Sophia," she sobbed. "I'm so sorry. I didn't even know. I just thought—"

"Hush." Her sister crossed back over to her. "You'll not blame any of this on yourself. You've been doing far too much of that lately as it is."

"But what you said, it's true. It will always be the same. Here you've finally found someone you love, and she's doing it again. She's taking both of us away just when we've—" Lydia halted, her brain fumbling over the words that desperately wanted to escape her lips.

Sophia's eyes probed hers. "Are you admitting that you love Caleb Jonas?"

Lydia sat in shock, half from the directness of Sophia's question and half from the question itself. Then she nodded. Her sister's slim arms were around her in an instant, giving her a healthy squeeze before releasing her. When Sophia retreated, Lydia detected a visible snap to her pale blue eyes.

"Then let's not," Sophia declared.

"Not?"

"We're not children. We can make our own decisions." Sophia stood with uncharacteristic forcefulness. "Why must Mother dictate our whole lives?"

Lydia watched in amazement as her sister paced the room. "I might as well tell you that Jim," she paused and flushed slightly at the use of his first name. "Jim has expressed his affection toward me. He's not wanted to push me because of the situation with Daddy. But Lydia." She turned and faced her. "He's asked me to marry him."

Lydia gave her a glad smile with watery eyes. "I'm so happy for you, Sissy. You deserve the best."

Sophia bounded back over to the bed and took hold of

Lydia's shoulders. "Don't you see? We can *both* stay."

A mere shake of her head was all Lydia could manage.

"But you just said that you love Caleb. What on earth—"

A pointed look from Lydia's eyes smothered the question. "I've pretty well pieced it together, Sophia. But you tell me. You were here last night, weren't you? When Caleb came? Now that I know Mother's plans, I can imagine what she said to him." She shook her head resignedly. "It would be foolish to even hope for anything."

"But Lydia," her sister pressed. "She's planning on going to San Francisco. And she even mentioned the possibility of. . ."

Lydia eyed her carefully and confirmed what she'd already suspected. "Ladies college," she finished for Sophia.

"You can't let her!"

"No, you were right the first time. It will never change. If you can possibly work things out for you and Jim, I'll be so happy for you." She dropped her gaze to the floor. "But I'm sure there's no chance that Caleb would come back here, not after whatever she planted in his mind last evening."

"Well," Sophia flailed her arms in emphatic circles. "Can't you meet him somewhere? Explain things to him?"

Lydia's chin hiked up a notch. "I'll do no such thing."

Sophia shook her head. "You know what your problem is, Miss Bennet? You and that bullheaded rancher are way too much alike."

Her words brought a smile to Lydia's glum face. "Maybe," she agreed. "But in spite of that, I know that I'll never marry someone else. I just couldn't."

❧

The day progressed as planned. Both of the Bennet girls packed, but each with a new destination in mind. Lydia convinced Sophia not to say anything to their mother until the last minute, hoping to avoid any fireworks over the remaining days. She'd need to be packed anyway when she joined Dr. Foy as his wife. He'd called later in the day, and when they had a moment away from her mother, Sophia had informed him of the situation and her answer to his proposal. Lydia noted that he'd left with a gleam in his twinkling blue eyes and that his dark moustache couldn't completely conceal the suppressed grin at their little secret. Lydia loved them—and envied them.

She herself had begun the job of packing for—she wasn't sure where. San Francisco? St. Augustine's Ladies College? She really didn't care. To be anywhere other than this place she'd fallen so completely in love with in such a short time. It housed too many memories of her foolishness, her father, and always. . .*him.*

She'd just finished helping Sophia clear away the supper dishes when a knock came at the back door. Assuming it was for Sophia, she winked at her slightly flustered sister and nodded toward the door. "Better let him in."

But a very different voice floated past her sister into the kitchen. Lydia dropped her dishcloth on the table as she watched Bradley Smyth breeze through the door. "Good evening, ladies."

Managing a polite smile, Lydia nodded in return.

"I'll tell Mother you're here," Sophia interjected. "She's in the parlor."

Smyth stood, his derby still in hand, smiling affably. Lydia, remembering some of her manners, took his hat and light jacket and hung them on the customary pegs in the hall. She didn't have the energy to invite him into the parlor, and she knew he'd follow her. So she simply started for the room.

Halfway there, they encountered her mother, who greeted the banker with pleasure. "Mr. Smyth. How lovely to see you."

"And you," he returned with a slight bow.

"Please, make yourself comfortable. If you'll excuse us for just a few moments, I'd like a word with Lydia before I retire for the evening."

"Certainly." He smiled and stepped down the hall.

Lydia followed her mother back into the kitchen. Her mother was short and to the point. "I'm sure that Sophia has related to you the arrangements that have been made for the upcoming days. Feel free to chat amiably with Mr. Smyth, but know that when the day after next arrives, we'll be on the stagecoach leaving Darby." She gave her daughter a direct look for emphasis and headed up the stairs.

Returning to her caller, Lydia instructed herself to be congenial if not entertaining. After all, the man had been nothing but friendly to her.

He grinned and rose from his chair when she entered the room. Sophia immediately took her leave. Finding a place on the settee, Lydia was horrified when Bradley joined her on the none-too-large piece of furniture.

"Lydia," his dark brown eyes gazed piercingly at hers. "I'm going to be a bit direct—perhaps err against decorum." He cleared his throat, and Lydia felt her own constrict.

"I'm aware after some business meetings with your mother that she's selling the mercantile and has plans to move—soon, I understand. I'd much rather do this in a more formal fashion, but the time doesn't allow."

Slipping his hand into his vest pocket, he retrieved a ring sporting a large, sparkling diamond surrounded by a circle of perfect pearls.

Lydia, shocked by not only the jewel but by the abruptness of his proposal, gasped and immediately regretted the action. She could only imagine what he would read into it. She certainly hadn't given him any encouragement.

"Mr. Smyth, I don't know what to say. I. . .I. . ."

He smiled with debonair confidence as he grasped her hand. "Bradley," he corrected her. "Now simply say yes." He began to slide the ring onto her finger.

Lydia jerked her hand back with more force than she'd intended.

His brow lowered into a slight frown. "What's the matter?"

"I. . .I just don't. . .I can't even begin. . ."

He grinned again, obviously mistaking her stutterings for some other overwhelming feeling.

"Lydia, darling. I know the last week has been trying. As I said, I didn't want to go about this in this way. But you must know, I'm intrigued by you. I can care for you. I can give you the world. You'll never want for anything. And we'll travel, we can—" His voice broke off as he studied her face.

Lydia pressed her lips together and averted her gaze. "Mr. Smy—"

"Bradley." His voice wasn't quite as endearing this time, an edge of impatience tainting it.

"Bradley," she faltered. "I sincerely appreciate your offer. You've been nothing but kind to me and my family—"

"But?"

She dared to raise her eyes to his. "But. . .do you love me?"

He stared at her, then chuckled. "Is that what this is all about? Is that what you want me to say? Okay. Lydia, I love you. Will you marry me?"

Lydia shook her head, smiling sadly. "No, Bradley. That's not it. That's not what I want to *hear.* That's what I want to *know.*"

His dark eyes took on a dangerous expression. "What are you talking about? I told you I love you. I've told you I'll care for you. What else do you want?"

What exactly do I want? Lydia stood from the settee and debated within herself. Finally she gave in. She'd be leaving in a few days. What did she have to lose? Perhaps expressing these ideas would make them more clear to her.

Tracing the edge of a book binding on a shelf, she began. "I want someone who understands. Someone to laugh with me, someone to watch the sun set and rise with me." She pulled the book from its place and absently flipped through the pages. "I want someone to read with, someone who'll bring to life all that I've read about and dreamed about—even if it's only in his imagination, too. Someone who knows. . ." Memories of her time spent with Caleb after he'd found her read like a bittersweet story in her mind. Those hours seemed of such lasting importance.

Suddenly she was aware of a nearby presence. With a sharp breath, she felt Bradley Smyth clutch tightly on her arm as he spun her around to face him. The look in his brown eyes was positively venomous. She'd never seen him so. . .so enraged.

As quickly as it had appeared, it vanished, and he self-consciously relinquished his grip, patting her arm almost in apology. "My dear," he said condescendingly. "You are young. I should have realized that. Of course you're going to harbor some of your storybook fantasies for a time. It's one of the things I find so charming about you.

"But in time, you'll learn. And understand." He unclenched his hand and revealed the ring. Undaunted, he again proceeded to push it into place on her finger.

This time, Lydia intercepted the ring, held it firmly, and pressed it just as determinedly back into his palm, closing his fingers around it. "But I do understand. I understand that I don't love you, and I refuse to settle for a marriage like that. I'm sorry." She forced herself to meet his face.

Surprisingly he merely dropped the piece of jewelry back into his vest pocket and looked at her for a long moment. Anger had been replaced by some emotion Lydia couldn't identify—and it terrified her.

"Alright, little lady." He took a step closer. His face was mere inches from hers.

She could feel every breath, but she steeled herself against his scornful glower. Somehow she felt it was important not to back down in spite of the fear making her backbone tingle.

"It's that lousy drifter, isn't it? That no-account rancher."

Lydia opened her mouth to respond, but her voice was nowhere to be found.

"Well, well." He stepped back. "I bid you good evening, Miss Bennet. It's been. . .enlightening." He started for the door. "I'll see myself out."

Lydia was sure she didn't breathe until she heard the click of the latch behind him. Then she all but collapsed. Grasping the bookshelves for support, she sagged against them heavily. "Oh, Lord. Help me."

fifteen

Bradley Smyth laid aside his quill and meticulously blotted the paper in front of him. After adding it to the neat stack, he stared at the sheets. It frustrated him that the normal pleasure he derived from such a business transaction was absent. In the end, he'd gotten what he wanted: Bennet's Mercantile. He hadn't counted on paying as much for it though.

If that belligerent Lydia Bennet hadn't waylaid his plans. . . Thoughts of her automatically led to bitter musings about Caleb Jonas. Smyth tapped his fingers forcefully against the desktop. That man had been a thorn in his side since coming to the area. First it had been his intrusion in Smyth's dealings with the new ranchers in the area. Bradley had prided himself in his ability to take over small ranches and farms when their occupants couldn't keep up with their loan payments.

Then in whisked this man from nowhere, and suddenly the loans were paid in full accompanied by notes saying, "Thank you, Mr. Smyth, but we no longer need the bank's services." Some checking into the background of the mysterious rancher showed nothing other than the fact that he'd originally been from the area, left after an accident claimed his family, moved to Texas, and had been a Texas Ranger for a time.

Bradley knew the corps wasn't paid enough to give a ranger the ability to bankroll several families. The money had to have come from somewhere. The where remained a mystery. What proved even more annoying was the man's reputation. He could ride the fastest, shoot the straightest, breed the best cattle, manage the best ranch. And then, of course, there was the subject of Lydia. Bradley hadn't been all that interested in her per se, but the fact that she, too, had opted for Jonas over himself. . .

Smyth clenched his eyes as he rubbed his temples. He

couldn't let the man get to him this way. Right now he had other problems to settle. Namely, Lydia Bennet.

The clock in the bank lobby chimed the hour just as a dusty Kid Cooley strode through the door. With his normal cockiness, he plopped into the upholstered chair facing Smyth.

Smyth eyed the layer of dirt covering the young man and shot him a disdainful glare. "Well, at least you're prompt. Your job will demand that."

Cooley smirked as he leaned his forearms on the shiny desktop. "And just what is my job this time, Mr. Banker?"

Smyth stood, retrieving the papers from the desk and filing them in the cabinet behind him. "Don't worry," he threw over his shoulder. "You'll enjoy it."

❧

"You sold the store? To Mr. Smyth?" Sophia's voice shattered the shocked silence. Lydia, for a change, was quiet.

Their mother continued to bustle around the sitting room, packing a few remaining items in a trunk sitting in the middle of the floor. "Who else would buy it?" she retorted. "Who would be able to?"

Sophia just shook her head. "I just thought. . .I thought you might advertise in some papers. Another family might be interested in moving here and taking over."

"Sophia, I do not have time for that. It's much simpler this way. Trust me." She placed the last book in the trunk and lowered the lid. "Now, you two better get to bed. The stage leaves early tomorrow. And Jeremy Crane, the blacksmith's assistant, has agreed to come and haul our luggage for us."

Lydia walked out the door, down the hall, and up the stairs, vaguely aware of the steps she was taking. Sophia joined her several minutes later and began her preparations for bed. As Lydia watched her sister brush out her long blond hair, she couldn't dislodge the lump in her throat. It was the last time she'd watch her do this. After tomorrow, Lydia would be gone, and Sophia would be someone's wife.

A tear slipped from her lashes just as Sophia turned. In an instant, her sister was at her side, giving her a reassuring hug.

No words were needed. They both knew. And the knowing silence made the beginning of their parting all the harder as they clung to one another in wordless misery.

After a time, they relinquished the embrace, and Sophia retired to her bed. Lydia wondered if her sister would be able to sleep, knowing the upcoming events. For herself, Lydia simply sat gazing out the window overlooking the main street of Darby, trying to take in each of its moonlit nuances one last time.

A sudden movement in the shadows of a nearby building caught her eye. She strained against the darkness to make out something.

Several minutes ticked by. Nothing.

Then she saw it again. This time a figure partially emerged. A man stepped cautiously into the street. The night's blackness hid his identity, leaving only the outline of his tall form visible.

Tilting her head to one side, she watched as he took a few steps toward the mercantile, slowed, then stopped altogether. He stood his ground for a heartbeat, then turned and began to stride away. Lydia's breath caught in her throat as she watched the shadowy figure place a Stetson atop his head.

❧

The bottom step outside the back door creaked in protest under her foot. Lydia winced. She'd managed to avoid all such spots on the stairs inside the house—even the door had been conspiratorially quiet. Glancing behind her, she shuffled around the building's side, suddenly aware of the coolness of the evening. But her destination gave her new purpose, and all apprehension vanished. He'd been there. He'd started to come to her. Her heart warmed. She would meet him halfway.

She cautiously picked her footing along the edge of the boardwalk, not daring to walk on its noisy planks. Her fingers idly ran along the hitching posts as she passed them. At last she came to the corner where she'd seen him. A narrow path led between two darkened houses.

Lydia hesitated for a moment. The path led to a back street that marked the edge of town. She turned and looked at the mercantile. The window she'd been sitting in was clearly visible, but she wasn't sure if she had been noticed from where she'd sat. In any event, it wasn't a long distance back home if he proved not to be there. But something told her he would.

She took the first step into the encroaching shadows of the two houses. Her pulse quickened, but she chided herself for being so anxious. If she could survive a night in the wilds on her own, she could certainly tackle a simple walk down a dark path.

She finally reached the edge of the path and in the meager moonlight that came and went with the passing of clouds, she searched one side of the back street and then the other. It was vacant. Her heart sank a few feet until she heard a noise behind her. Spinning around, she saw a figure leaning against the house. Her stomach fluttered as she watched the Stetson tip back on his head. "Caleb?" she breathed.

Pushing away from the clapboard siding, he sauntered toward her and removed his hat altogether.

"Sorry." The unexpected voice made her throat go dry just as the moon reappeared and revealed his identity. "Hope I'll do instead."

His sinister tone was not lost on her, and Lydia shuddered. The lump in her throat seemed too large to swallow around, much less speak through. "What do you want?" she croaked.

Cooley's eyes narrowed at the same time his lips curled into a tight little smile. "Ohhh, I thought I'd just see if the Kid would be an okay stand-in for Mr. Bigshot Rancher." He extended his index finger and ran it up and down her bare arm. "Did a pretty good job, didn't I? Gotcha out here anyway."

She took a step back, leaving his finger trailing in midair. "Mr. Cooley." She tried to speak with more forcefulness than her shaking body actually possessed. "I am going home. Good night." She took a step to the side and tried to pass him.

His strong hand gripped her arm midstride. "I don't think so."

Her eyes widened. Before she could even gasp, he yanked

her forcefully toward him and began nuzzling his face in her neck. His fingers fumbled with the buttons of her dress.

Dear God, she pleaded inwardly, *save me.*

Knowing she had to do something, Lydia cried out in the night air, but before she could manage a scream, he brandished a glistening blade. "Don't get any bright ideas, missy, or you're liable to lose your tongue altogether."

Shaking like a leaf, Lydia froze in horror as he placed the tip of the knife against her heart. She closed her eyes and prayed for the end to come quickly. Instead she heard and felt the blade slowly cutting down the center of her dress's bodice. Shaky little sobs began to overtake her again. "Please don't," she spoke in a wavery voice. "Please."

He chuckled.

Lydia felt her knees begin to weaken.

"I think it would be in your best interest to drop that knife."

Lydia started.

Kid Cooley whirled around.

Her eyes fluttered open to see a stocky figure outlined at the opposite end of the path. Her heart tripped over itself in relief. "Caleb!"

"Shut up!" Cooley grabbed her arm and, twisting it painfully, dragged her in front of him, his knife pressing uncomfortably against her neck.

Lydia watched as Caleb continued to move closer. With each step he took, the blade pinched tighter against her throat.

"You're doin' a good job of ordering her funeral, Jonas. Back off."

Cooley's warning had no effect on Caleb's approach. "Come on, Cooley. You're more of a man than that, aren't you? Using a woman to hide behind? Let's settle this man to man. Let her go."

"Take another step, man. Just try it." A flick of his wrist caused the tip of the knife to slice against Lydia's jawline. She cried out in pain and closed her eyes as warm drops of blood trickled onto her shoulder where her bodice had been torn away.

Caleb halted. "Okay, okay. I'm staying put. Just put down the knife."

Lydia could feel Kid Cooley's chest heaving against her back in short, sporadic breaths.

"Yeah," Kid laughed, his voice a trifle high. "Yeah. Maybe I will get rid of this thing."

Lydia dared to open her eyes and saw the knife waving perilously close to her face. She felt Cooley fumbling with something else behind her. Suddenly she knew.

"Caleb!" she shouted.

In an instant, Kid Cooley shoved her aside, sending her sprawling against the house.

She tried to gain some sort of foothold, anything, but it was all in vain. Everything seemed to be happening in slow motion.

Deafening shots echoed around her. As she crumpled to the ground, she felt her head hit something. Piercing pain rammed through her skull. Darkness swallowed her up.

sixteen

Caleb gazed down at the gun in his hand. This hadn't actually happened, had it? He replayed the last minutes of the evening, wondering if perhaps it were all a bad dream. He'd stayed on in town, knowing Lydia was leaving. He'd battled over whether to storm her home and set the situation between them to rights. . .or leave it alone. Unfortunately he'd opted for inaction.

He moved his feet almost mechanically toward the body lying the short distance in front of him. Kid Cooley's fixed, unseeing stare told Caleb all he needed to know. The young man's gun hadn't cleared his holster, but it was obvious that he'd tried. The thong had slipped loose and the gun hung out, askew. And the knife he'd brandished lay off to the side. As Caleb averted his eyes from the body, conflicting emotions of relief and regret charged back and forth within his soul. Hadn't he left Texas to get away from this very thing?

A moan from nearby made his head jerk up, suddenly aware of his surroundings again.

Holstering his pistol, he ran to where Lydia lay in a crumpled heap. He dropped to his knees, trying to make out the features of her face. A cut on her jawline was swollen and had, it seemed, ceased bleeding for the most part, although it left its telltale mark down her neck in dried, darkened streaks.

Anger seethed through Caleb. So the wretch *had* cut her. In the shadows of the night he'd not been able to tell. He'd only heard her cry out, and he'd hoped it was from fear. At least the wound had closed. Somewhat relieved, he gently cradled her head in his hands. "Lydia?" he murmured.

There was no response.

He tried to raise her shoulders a little. "Come on, Lydia."

Her head rolled slowly toward his chest, and his heart lurched within him at the sight of a deep gash sliced across the left side of her forehead. A dark crimson stain was flowing steadily down into her hair and neck. "Oh, dear God. . ."

Stinging tears blurred his vision, and he pulled her closer, lowering his face near hers. A barely detectable breath feathered across his cheek. The tears fell unheeded down his cheeks. "Oh, God," he petitioned in a hoarse whisper. "Please don't let her die. I know I haven't the right to ask anything of You, but I have to. She's one of Yours, God. Don't let her die. Please. . ."

He stroked his thumb over the softness of her cheek. Then ever so gently, he eased her into his arms and stood. He needed to get her to Doc Foy's. Now.

❧

Bradley had watched in horror as his plan slowly unraveled before his eyes. That fool kid, what had he been thinking? A lump of frustration mixed with a healthy dose of fear stuck in his throat as he slumped against the rough siding of the nearby building. He'd instructed the buffoon just to scare her a little bit. That's when he had planned to step into the picture. The great hero. Perhaps then she would have seen things his way.

But now, he recoiled in terror. As if Kid's overzealous behavior wasn't enough. . . What was Jonas doing in town anyway? Bradley had started just as much as the Kid when Jonas's voice had split the silence of the night. A distinct feeling of dread washed over him. This had not worked out at all like he'd planned. It was entirely too messy now.

He'd been trying to work through the intricacies of the problem when the shot rang out. Stunned, he ducked back several steps, hunkering down against the side of the building, hoping that no stray bullets would come his way. Whether the time seemed short or long, he couldn't really tell. But when the last shot's ringing echo had finally faded away, he took several shallow breaths, attempting to fill his lungs. When he felt like he'd regained some stability, he dared a peek around the corner. Of the three people he'd been watching, one remained standing. In spite of the darkness, Bradley knew who that was.

A sick feeling washed over him. What had he gotten himself into? Quick thoughts of alibis chased through his agitated mind. But wait. If Kid Cooley was dead, who would be the wiser?

Slinking back, Smyth readied himself an escape. He could act as surprised as the rest when the news came out. It was well known that there had been tension between Jonas and Cooley. He smiled. Of course. Jonas and Cooley.

His grin broadened as a new plan formed. At last, it was *his* time. But he had to move quickly. All too soon the ruckus would bring at least a few townspeople out to investigate.

Stepping out from his concealed place, he made his presence known with thundering steps and an imposing entrance. "Jonas! What's going on?"

The rancher whirled around at the sound of the voice. Surprise, then relief registered in his voice. "Smyth? Is that you? Help me here. We've got to get Lydia over to Doc's. Fast! She's bleeding bad."

Bradley approached warily at first, then pressed on with renewed fortitude. "Here, give her to me. You look a little shaken." He pulled a handkerchief from his pocket and tossed it at Caleb. "Put that on her wound." He slid his arms around Lydia's limp form and eased her weight onto his own.

"Got her?" Caleb inquired.

Smyth nodded. "Why don't you go check on him." He pointed with his head toward Kid Cooley's lifeless body.

"I did. There's not much that can be done for him, I'm afraid."

Before Bradley could respond, a raft of voices wafted across the night air, growing louder by the second. A small group of townsfolk gathered on the scene, their nightclothes hastily covered with outer wraps.

"What's going on? What were the shots? Who's out here?" The general cacophony of questions drowned itself out.

More than a few gasps were heard as individuals discovered the body lying on the dirt street. Stewart Cleary, the blacksmith, was the first to reach the body. "It's that Cooley kid," he shouted back to the others. The pronouncement was met with more gasps and clucking tongues.

The crowd had grown, and Doc Foy had joined the throng. Judging the situation he swiftly concluded that the young woman in Smyth's arms was the priority.

Lydia was ushered into yet another waiting pair of arms while some of the other townsmen took the job of retrieving the body of the young cowboy. The crowd fell in step behind the doctor, who was closely followed by Sheriff Watkins. The portly lawman fell back and approached Smyth and Caleb.

"I'd like you fellows to follow us," he informed them. "I need to ask you both a few questions."

Caleb nodded in morose silence.

"Of course," Smyth agreed. "I'd be happy to answer your questions, Sheriff. I saw *everything.*" He slid a sidelong glance at Caleb before quickening his pace to rejoin the front of the crowd.

❧

Caleb paced the dimly lit parlor of Doc Foy's house, completely oblivious to the others who were waiting for news. The only time his head had popped up in recognition was when Mrs. Bennet and Sophia had been ushered in. They'd looked rather sleepy and bewildered. He couldn't imagine how they could comprehend this latest turn of events.

When at last the doctor emerged from the patient's quarters, Caleb had to restrain himself from rushing forward. Although he felt a real and tangible part of him lay in that adjoining room, teetering on the edge of life, the memory of his conversation with Mrs. Bennet weighed heavily on his heart and mind. He kept his distance, allowing the concerned family their space.

Mrs. Bennet approached the doctor, her face stoic, seemingly preparing herself for the worst. Caleb watched as Jim Foy placed his hands on the woman's shoulders and gave

Sophia a compassionate look.

"Lydia is alive."

That comment in itself brought several sighs of relief from throughout the room. Caleb felt the weight within his chest lift just a fraction.

"She has lost a lot of blood. The wound to her head was severe, and judging from the symptoms, I'm afraid she may have some internal bruising."

Mrs. Bennet's hand flew to her mouth. Sophia's eyes brimmed over with tears.

Dr. Foy flicked a glance at the floor before returning to meet their gazes. "She is not conscious."

As Mrs. Bennet's lower lip began to quiver, Sophia released a stifled sob.

Caleb froze. He watched as if in slow motion Doc held the two women. "I'm doing everything I can," he heard Doc murmur.

An incessant buzzing reverberated through Caleb's head. He tried to shake it clear, but it grew worse. Squeezing his eyes shut, he tried to regain his mental footing. The blackness began to lighten, fuzzy images formulated. Lydia. Kid Cooley. His own gun, blazing in his hand. Blood streaming from her head, falling onto his hands.

His eyes flew open. Slowly raising his hands from his sides, he studied them in revulsion. A sick feeling heaved through him. They were covered with dried, brown patches of blood. Hers.

Wiping them feverishly against his pants, he suddenly became aware of the other voices around him once again.

Apparently while he'd been preoccupied with his own thoughts, Doc Foy had officially announced Kid Cooley's death. A new feeling of trepidation fell over Caleb. A tap on his shoulder made him jump. He turned to find Sheriff Watkins standing beside him. "Would you come with me, Jonas?"

The sudden intrusion into his thoughts made him stare blankly at the man for a moment. "I. . .sure." Caleb shot a look in Doc Foy's direction. He desperately wanted to confer with the doctor about Lydia's injuries. He returned his attention to Watkins. "Couldn't I just answer your questions here?"

The sheriff averted his gaze. "I'm afraid not."

Caleb blinked. "Why not?"

"You will be answering some questions, Caleb. But I'm afraid it will be done down at the jail."

"What?" Caleb's response was almost drowned out by several shocked gasps from the group about the room.

"I'll need your gun, too."

Caleb stood, chagrined.

Watkins shifted his weight to his other foot, obviously uncomfortable with the situation. "Your gun." He held out his hand expectantly.

"Sheriff," Caleb started to interject. "I understand your need to ask questions and all but why the—"

"Are you denying that you shot Kid Cooley?" The cold voice emerged from somewhere behind the sheriff. Caleb saw Bradley Smyth ease out of the crowd, his dark eyes challenging.

Caleb leveled his own unwavering gaze. "No, I'm not. But—"

"And you're not denying that the reason you were out there tonight was to see Lydia?"

A warning bell sounded in Caleb's brain. He looked skeptically at his accuser. "I saw her—" He stopped. "I was concerned about her."

Smyth took a step forward. "Seems a trifle strange way to show concern, holding her at knifepoint."

If Caleb did his best to hold his own shock in check, none of the other onlookers did. A murmur of voices began to rise around him.

"What are you talking about?" An agitated voice came from Caleb's right. He saw Jim Foy marching to his side. "That cut was made by Cooley's knife." More murmurs—apparently some folks hadn't known about the gash from the blade. But through it all, Caleb kept his eyes trained on Smyth's face.

"Right," the banker agreed. "Which, of course, was easily accessible after Kid Cooley was dead."

It took every ounce of strength Caleb possessed not to lunge after this snake masquerading as a man. Of course. It was all falling neatly and horribly into place. He'd been so preoccupied with Lydia that he hadn't been aware of Smyth's furtiveness. He should have known. He'd been the first one to the scene. It had seemed a little more than coincidental.

"Jonas?"

Caleb directed his attention to the sheriff.

"Have you anything to say on this matter?"

Looking the lawman straight in the eye, his voice did not falter. "I shot Kid Cooley." His eyes returned to the black stare of Smyth. "I was trying to save Lydia. And Cooley had grabbed for his gun." Again, undertones of conversation.

"Interesting," Smyth declared. "I thought someone said his gun was still in the holster."

The babble of voices rose to a near deafening pitch.

The sheriff hollered several times to quiet things down. "I'm sorry, Jonas. But you're going to have to come with me. I've reasonable evidence to bring you in. And you've freely admitted to shooting Kid Cooley. The rest we'll have to wait on."

A painful lump formed in Caleb's throat. "The rest?"

Sheriff Watkins merely glanced at Dr. Foy. "Keep me posted on Miss Bennet's condition." With a nod in the direction of the door, he indicated for Caleb to go with him.

Caleb turned toward his doctor friend, noting the confused and concerned expression he wore. And then he saw the chilling wrath of Mary Bennet.

seventeen

Caleb shifted his weight for the hundredth time on the stiff, unresisting wooden plank that served as the tiny cell's cot. A few threadbare blankets were of little use, although the amount of dirt on them indicated previous inmates had hoped otherwise.

Slapping his hands against his thighs, he stood and began to pace the meager space. He'd been there only a few hours, and already he was going mad. If only he had something to look at, read, anything. As if he'd be able to concentrate, he thought grimly. The last twelve hours kept playing through his mind in a maddening circle. He should have gotten knocked on the head. Then he wouldn't be sitting in this roach-infested jail.

That realization brought immediate self-reproach. Yes, he'd gladly have taken that bump on his head. Simply to save poor Lydia. When he thought of her lying limp and pale on the brink of death, he was filled with a hollow, sick feeling. Why couldn't he have stayed away from her in the first place?

The only sounds that broke the irritating silence were the intermittent jangle of keys and scraping of chair legs against the wood floor from the front room. Caleb grasped the iron bars in front of him and leaned against them heavily. His thoughts were in such a tangle. Was there a purpose for all of this? Was this the way his life was supposed to end?

Somewhere from the long forgotten recesses of his memory came his father's voice. In spite of the ten years since Jeremiah Jonas's voice had been silenced, his well-modulated teacher's intonation washed over Caleb's mind as if he'd heard him just yesterday: *Life is full of choices, Son. You can decide where and when you want to go. But you need to realize most importantly that if we trust in the Lord, He will direct our steps. No matter where our foolish inclinations may lead us, He'll work things out for good. He's true to His Word.*

Caleb frowned at the recollection. He'd grown up listening to both of his parents not only read the Bible, but actually live it out in their lives. As a boy, he'd taken in every word, accepting it at face value. But as he grew older, he'd begun to question whether all the words were applicable to his life. He'd never strayed very far from the moral teachings that had been instilled in him. But neither had he embraced the life that his parents had prayed he would.

Now for the first time in a long while, he replayed many of the things that had never quite been erased from his memory. They offered him comfort, if nothing else.

A sudden squeak from the front office made Caleb's head jerk. He gripped the bars, peering to see who might have come. In the interchange with the deputy, Caleb recognized Willy Albert's voice. He couldn't remember when he'd been so happy to see the grizzled old bunkhouse cook. He greeted his visitor with a slight smile. Willy was unusually quiet. He had trouble meeting Caleb's eye.

Caleb finally broke the uncomfortable silence. "It's good to see you, Willy."

A nod. "Couldn't very well stay away now, could I?" He cleared his throat and shuffled his feet.

"Everything okay at the ranch?"

Another nod.

"Men are keeping up?"

Willy's head dipped again.

Caleb stared at the man's averted face. "Are you gonna' talk to me?" A tangible feeling of grief suddenly came over him. "Or do you think I did it, too?"

"Course not!" the answer fairly exploded forth. "Ain't no one in their right mind that would figure that."

"I hope so." Caleb stepped back to sit on the hard cot.

He eyed the package in Willy's arms. "Whatcha got there?"

Willy stared back blankly, then followed Caleb's gaze. "Oh, shucks. Nearly fergot! Got some bread and a few other goodies in here." He handed the paper sack through the bars.

Caleb gratefully took it and immediately began rifling through its contents. "Thanks! I just realized how hungry I was."

His visitor sat in companionable silence. As Caleb tore a bite off the roast beef sandwich, he stole a glance back at his longtime friend. "Have you heard any more about Lydia?"

Willy slowly shook his head, a sad, understanding look on his face.

As he chewed mechanically, Caleb suddenly realized the food no longer held much appeal. He swallowed around the thickness in his throat and washed it down with a dipper of water from the bucket provided him. He stuffed the rest into the bag for later.

After several minutes it was painfully obvious that there wasn't much to say. But Caleb was simply grateful for the companionship. After a time, Willy finally stood. "Well, I'd best be gettin' back."

Caleb stood with him and gave a resigned nod in answer.

Willy cleared his throat before turning toward the door. "I'll keep prayin' for you."

Caleb stared after him, trying to ignore the emptiness he felt inside.

Later that day, the sheriff stopped in. He seemed quiet, and Caleb noticed the man also seemed reluctant to meet his eye.

"Thought I'd let you know, they've set the trial for tomorrow."

Caleb nodded.

"Smyth was going to bring in one of them high-priced, fast-talkin' eastern lawyers. I assured him that since he wasn't directly involved with Cooley or the Bennets, it wasn't necessary."

A small feeling of relief washed over Caleb at that news.

The sad, gray eyes of the older man looked pointedly at Caleb. "But you'll be on your own on that stand."

"I know."

"Okay. Just. . .be careful up there."

Caleb gave the man a half smile. He knew the lawman was behind him. He believed him. But the warning in his tone and eyes was evident: *Watch out for Smyth.*

The afternoon ticked by sluggishly. Caleb had managed to coax a newspaper from the deputy, simply to have something to do to pass the time. He nibbled on the food brought by Willy and tried to forget what the morning would bring. He did have the presence of mind to ask to be brought a clean set of clothes, and he was hoping he'd be able to shave at some point.

Near dusk, the door to the small jail creaked again.

Assuming it was the deputy's relief for the night, Caleb continued to read the paper for the fourth time.

"You up on all the news, Jonas?"

His head snapped up at the greeting. Jim Foy stood at the entrance of the small room.

Caleb rose and crossed to the bars. "Hey, Doc. Good to see you."

"And you." The doctor's keen blue eyes studied Caleb carefully. "Sophia wanted to accompany me, but she thought it best not to make too many waves with her mother right now. And she didn't really want to leave Lydia."

Caleb's stance perked up. "Has she come to?"

Foy threw a glance at the floor, hesitating before slowly shaking his head.

The slump immediately returned to Caleb's shoulders.

The doctor pulled up a nearby chair and sat next to the cell. "I can't stay very long. I want to be back when Lydia wakes up."

His use of the word *when* didn't escape Caleb's notice, and he appreciated his friend's compassion.

"Jonas, have you ever read the Bible?"

"A long time ago."

"Well, I've brought one for you. Thought it might help pass the time."

Caleb grasped the proffered book as Jim pushed it between the bars.

"Caleb," his friend hesitated before continuing. "Have you ever wondered why all this is happening to you?"

"You've no idea."

Jim Foy leaned over, his arms resting on his legs as he peered intently at Caleb. "I think I do. But what I want to know is if you're prepared for the battle to come."

Caleb turned on his heel and paced back and forth. "I don't know," he finally admitted. "It seems like it's already done. I mean, given the circumstances, what chance do I have?"

Jim didn't answer immediately. His eyes squinted in concentration, his moustache twitching while he nibbled his lower lip. "I was kind of afraid that was how you were feeling."

Caleb whirled around. "Do you blame me?"

"No." Foy stood and approached the bars, placing his hands on them much as Caleb had done earlier. "But I don't want you to give up either."

Caleb averted his stony gaze to another part of the cell.

The doctor cleared his throat. "Have you ever read about Caleb in the Bible?"

A vague recollection swirled in his memory, but nothing stood out. "Nothing I remember."

Jim nodded. "I've taken the liberty of marking a few passages in that Bible. If you have time, read them."

Caleb's eyes finally met his friend's, and he gave a wry smile. "Okay, I'll see if I can find time."

Foy's blue eyes contained a hint of their familiar spark. "Take care, friend. We'll see you tomorrow." He reached for Caleb's hand and clutched it firmly. Suddenly Caleb didn't feel quite so alone.

❧

The supper hour had come and gone. Caleb shoved his empty plate near the bars where the deputy could retrieve it. The last fragments of light were fast slipping under the cover of darkness. He glanced at the outline of the book lying on his cot. He desperately wanted to read it. But now. . .

A few seconds later, the deputy entered to fetch the plate, and Caleb intercepted him before he could walk away.

"Hey, would it be possible to get a lantern or a candle or something in here?"

"Nope. You're not allowed those things in the cell. Rules. Might try and start a fire or something."

Caleb's heart sunk several inches. His disappointment must have inspired some pity in the young deputy. He glanced around and finally said, "Well, I might be able to put one on a table just outside the cell. The light won't be the best, but—"

"That would be fine!" Caleb smiled as the man walked away.

True to his word, the deputy dug up a meager candle and placed it on a rickety little table, just out of Caleb's reach. Caleb had to lean against the bars, holding the book so it would catch the flickering light. It was nowhere near comfortable, and at first he considered forgetting the whole notion. But as he delved into the passages in Numbers and Joshua that the doctor had marked, he found himself too caught up in the story to stop.

He read about when Moses and the Israelites were about to come into this new land, a land promised to flow with milk and honey. But they faced one big obstacle: huge strong men already lived there. The Israelites had to take the whole place from them. Caleb was amazed how most of them wanted to run back to Egypt where they'd been slaves. What a bunch of foolish folks. And only Joshua and Caleb were ready to go.

As he read, Caleb noted that a few verses were underlined: *Surely they shall not see the land which I sware unto their father, neither shall any of them that provoked me see it; But my servant Caleb, because he had another spirit with him, and hath followed me fully, him will I bring into the land whereinto he went; and his seed shall possess it.*

In other passages, he read how Caleb devoted himself to the Lord and in return the Lord gave him the strength to overcome, along with the promise of an inheritance of this new land filled with his offspring.

A light finally came on in his mind, one that had shown brightly as a youth and had faded away when he'd turned from God. Placing the book on the cot, Caleb knelt on the cold wood floor and poured out his heart to God. "Lord, I finally understand. I know that You are in control. I still have a lot of questions. But I pray You will keep me next to You so I won't be like the Israelites who wanted to go back to being slaves.

"I'm painfully aware that I don't deserve any of the grace You've given me. It's pretty clear to me that I've made a mess of things.

"God, I don't know where this whole situation is leading me. Your promise of inheritance to that Caleb may not necessarily be mine. He followed You completely. I haven't. And I'm paying for the path I chose for myself. I just pray from here on out, Your will be done."

An indescribable peace spread over him. And in the darkness of that little cell, he finally let go. His grief and bitterness over losing his parents and brother, his painful memories of watching his fellow rangers die in the line of duty, the intense and confusing feelings he'd never encountered before meeting Miss Lydia Bennet. The guilt and regret of shooting Kid Cooley, and perhaps most of all, his hatred of Bradley Smyth.

With each silent tear that slipped down his cheeks, he shed it all. Close to the light of morning, Caleb Jonas sank onto the cot and slept soundly for the first time in many, many years.

eighteen

Day did come, only not with its usual late summer exuberance. No fingers of sunshine reached out to coax awake a sleeping world. Dismal gray clouds hung in clumps low to the ground, blanketing everything in a chilling mist.

Caleb awoke with a shiver and pulled one of the ratty blankets tighter around him. He'd been sleeping so soundly he'd nearly forgotten where he was. But the roughness of the pine slab beneath his head quickly brought it all back.

Easing himself up into a sitting position, he groaned as he tried to work the kinks out of his back and neck. From the front room he smelled the pungent aroma of fresh brewed coffee, but instead of setting his stomach to rumbling, it did nothing more than send a queasiness through his being. Taking a deep breath and exhaling slowly, he lifted a quick petition heavenward. "Oh, God. Give me the strength to get through this," he whispered.

One of the young deputies approached carrying a basin of steaming water and some fresh clothes. Caleb eyed the water appreciatively as it was placed in his cell. "Say, is there a chance I might be able to shave?" His fingers kneaded the almost two-day-old growth covering his face.

"I don't think so. A razor is another one of those off-limits items."

Promptly the sheriff marched in. "Mornin', Jonas."

Caleb nodded politely, keenly aware that with each new law officer present his day of reckoning was closer to its beginning.

"Need a shave, do we?" Sheriff Watkins eased into a congenial smile.

"But, Sheriff," the deputy interjected. "There's not supposed to be any—"

"I'll take full responsibility, Deputy Tanner. I think we can trust the man with a shave." He brought out a folded razor and a cake of soap.

Caleb could do nothing more than smile his heartfelt appreciation. He quickly went to the work of stripping off the dirty, bloodstained shirt and liberally splashing the refreshing water over his face, neck, and chest.

All the while he bathed, shaved, changed his clothes, and finally slicked back his wet hair, his thoughts kept jumping ahead to the day that lay before him.

As a ranger, he'd been involved in enough trials that he knew what to expect. The difference was that he'd always been called upon as a mere witness. He had known nothing about how the accused had felt. And admittedly, he hadn't cared. But now he faced something he never thought would happen to him in a hundred years. He was being tried for the murder of a man he'd shot in self-defense and the attempted murder of a woman he loved desperately.

He tried to replay all that had transpired the night and early morning hours before. Though the former heaviness was gone, he realized his dread was not. He knew the Lord would sustain him, no matter what. But his flesh desperately cried out for mercy. Men had been hung for lesser things than this. That thought sent a terrifying shudder through him. It wasn't that he feared dying itself, but his thoughts kept flashing to a vulnerable, poignant face set with green eyes and framed with fiery red curls. Who would take care of Lydia?

❧

The appointed hour had come. Sheriff Watkins approached the cell, his round face glum. Before he led Caleb from the dismal quarters, he apologized with his eyes as he placed the shackles about Caleb's wrists. Caleb merely nodded, conveying in silence that he understood. He didn't hold it against the man.

The day had not brightened any, and when the two stepped from the small jailhouse, wind pelted tiny drops of rain against their faces. But as dreary as the weather was, Caleb would have gladly stayed in it rather than approach the schoolhouse.

His mind flashed to the last time he'd been there. John Bennet's funeral. Part of him swore he'd never step inside the little building again as long as he lived. *As long as he lived.* He nearly laughed at the irony of that thought.

Once again, the little structure was filled to near bursting. He tried to ignore the stares and murmurs when he was escorted into the room. The whole town was there, and then some. Up in front, the desk had been made into a bench for the judge who resided over this section of the territory. He sat there in his unofficial-looking garb, and Caleb wondered what he did for a living when he wasn't convicting people.

Also near the front he spotted Mary and Sophia Bennet, flanked by Bradley Smyth and Dr. Foy. Caleb considered it unusual for parties in such separate camps to be seated next to each other. But then, he wasn't entirely sure where Sophia stood on the issue of his innocence.

Caleb was guided to a seat near the front, off to one side and facing the judge's bench. When he was seated, a bang of the gavel got the trial underway. The ricocheting echoes rung in his ears for a long time.

The first to the stand was Sheriff Watkins. He merely presented the evidence as he'd collected it. As impartial as the lawman tried to be, Caleb had to flinch when he heard it all strung together. It didn't sound good at all.

The next to the stand was Doc Foy. As he raised his hand and placed the other on the Bible, his gaze didn't waver, nor did his voice. The judge proceeded.

"Dr. Foy, can you tell me the exact injuries sustained by Bertram Cooley?"

"Yes. Bertram Cooley died from a gunshot wound directly to the heart. Death was instantaneous." A few murmurs moved across the room.

"And the injuries sustained by Miss Lydia Bennet?"

"Miss Bennet incurred a superficial knife wound to her jawline, a smattering of bruises on her arms, a severe blow to the upper corner of her forehead which has rendered her unconscious, and a possible bruising of the brain."

A loud sniff came from the front row. Caleb couldn't bring himself to see if it had come from Sophia or her mother.

"Thank you, Doctor. You may take your seat." The judge scribbled down a few notes before lifting his eyes.

"Sheriff Watkins, would you retake the stand, please?"

The lawman dutifully complied, albeit slowly. Caleb noticed he seemed tired.

"Sheriff, do you concur that the bullet taken from Bertram Cooley's body was indeed one fired from Caleb Jonas's gun?"

"Yes, sir. A Colt .45 Peacemaker, rechambered to fit the .44 Winchester rifle cartridge."

"And the knife involved belonged to. . .?"

"The knife appeared to belong to Kid—Bertram Cooley, sir."

"Thank you, Sheriff. You may step down."

A few more murmurs filtered through the crowd, and Caleb noticed the judge casting a somber eye across the room. Nearly all the noise ceased.

"I'm going to proceed to call upon character witnesses. When I call your name, please approach the bench. You will be sworn in, and I will ask you a few questions." He glanced down at his sheet before lifting his eyes to the crowd. "Dr. Jim Foy."

Jim Foy retook the stand.

"I remind you, Doctor, you're still under oath."

"I understand."

Caleb watched as his friend sat straight and confident, secretly wishing the doctor could send some of that feeling his way. So far, it had taken all his strength just to resist flinging his head into his hands in misery.

"Doctor, you are acquainted in an unofficial capacity with Caleb Jonas, correct?"

"Yes, that's correct. I would say we're close friends."

"Stating as such, are you of the opinion that Mr. Jonas

could have committed these crimes?"

"Sir, as I'm sure you're aware, Caleb has confessed to shooting Bertram Cooley in self-defense. As far as the other charge, I see no way that he would be capable of such an act."

A nod released the doctor from the chair, and Caleb caught his friend's eye before he was seated. He hoped Jim could read his thanks.

Several other witnesses were called. A few businessmen from Darby, a handful of his ranch hands, Willy—all attested to the fact that they couldn't imagine Caleb being responsible for such a crime.

After all that testimony, Caleb was beginning to feel the odds might be in his favor.

"Mrs. John Bennet."

Mary Bennet's slim form stepped toward the chair, and in a wavery voice, she swore to tell the truth.

"Mrs. Bennet, can you tell me how long you've known Mr. Jonas?"

She gave an imperious nod. "We met him shortly after moving here in May. So it's been only a few months."

"I see. And from what you know of him, would you consider him capable of committing the crimes for which he has been charged?"

Mary Bennet's piercing blue eyes looked directly at Caleb in icy contempt. "I most certainly do!"

A loud cacophony of voices rose above the throng. Several bangs of the gavel did little to alleviate the tension.

After order was restored, the judge continued. "Can you tell me why you believe as you do?"

"Well, first of all he was a Texas Ranger. No one else would have been able to shoot with such accuracy. But as far as Lydia. . ." For a moment her voice nearly broke, but she swallowed and began again. "He was trying to pursue my Lydia. But I told him that it wasn't in her best interest to be involved with a person such as he."

Caleb stared at the floor, remembering all too well the humiliating evening in the Bennet's parlor. Now the whole town would know, too.

"He became very upset with me. And he threatened me."

At that, Caleb's head flew up. He had what?

"Threatened you, Mrs. Bennet? Physically?"

"Well," she cast her gaze to the hankie she toyed with in her gloved hands. "No." Her chin jutted back up. "But he threatened to ruin me financially. To give me a bad name."

Caleb closed his eyes as he remembered his comments about her gossiping. Had she stretched that for all it was worth!

"Thank you, Mrs. Bennet. No further questions."

Caleb let out a ragged breath as she was dismissed.

"Uh, next is. . ." The judge referred to his paper. "Sophia Bennet."

As he bit his lower lip, Caleb prayed for Sophia. She looked exhausted. Her pale complexion was heightened by the circles under her eyes—ones that hadn't been there in a long time. Until he had—

Enough, he chastised himself. *How long will you blame yourself for everything?* But he couldn't shake the feeling that he seemed to be at the root of a lot of this.

Sophia was asked the same questions as everyone else. She spoke in her quiet but confident voice. No, she didn't believe Caleb to be the cause of her sister's injuries. Yes, she believed he was a good man and truly cared for her sister in spite of what had transpired between him and her mother.

Gratitude filled Caleb's heart as Sophia stepped down from the chair and rejoined Dr. Foy. Her mother, he noticed, had a stiff set to her jaw and avoided looking at her daughter.

The last witness called was the first witness on the scene, Bradley Smyth. Caleb started to get nervous. He clenched his eyes and prayed God would rejuvenate his spirit.

Smyth had chosen one of his finest suits for the occasion, almost it seemed, in a celebratory manner. He, too, took the oath and settled himself comfortably in the witness chair. He was totally in his element.

"Mr. Smyth, do you feel Mr. Jonas is responsible for the crimes in question?"

"Absolutely."

Caleb's gut flinched, although he'd been expecting the answer.

"Can you tell me why?"

"Well, I'd have to reiterate what Mrs. Bennet said about Mr. Jonas being a marksman. As for Lydia, excuse me, Miss Bennet. . ."

The feigned slip didn't go unnoticed by Caleb, and his blood started to boil.

"I had witnessed on several occasions the rivalry between Mr. Jonas and Mr. Cooley. The summer picnic, for one. I'm sure others of you recall." He waved his hand over the crowded room, playing them like an easy deck of cards.

Caleb could only sit in amazement as he watched this man smoothly turn the tables and run the show without the judge or anyone else being aware of it.

"It seems fairly clear, doesn't it?" the banker challenged. "Mr. Jonas wanted to possess Miss Bennet. She simply wasn't interested. First she ran from him. Then when he went after her, he thought he'd have some time to woo her back."

The empty, sick feeling inside Caleb was fast being replaced by pure hatred. To think he had prayed for this man the night before! What had happened to his peace? Where was it now?

Smyth's smooth voice droned on. "But her father's death changed all that as well. And now you have a bitter man who, angered by what he couldn't have, vowed that if he couldn't have her, no one else would either."

Caleb jumped to his feet. "That is a bald-faced lie!" he spat venomously.

Smyth's eyes betrayed nothing.

"Mr. Jonas!" the judge commanded. "Be seated. I'll not have you disrupting this court like that again. I assure you, your opportunity to refute these charges will come."

Caleb took a deep breath and took his seat. All the while, his glare never left the banker's face, but it gave him no satisfaction. Tilting his head in sudden curiosity, Caleb realized that not once had Smyth looked at him. He'd looked everywhere else in the room but at him. A new thought occurred to Caleb: Smyth was scared stiff. Not of lying, but of being caught in it by Caleb.

Smyth at last stepped down, and Caleb waited to be called to the stand. When at last he was, he stepped to the chair. The deputy brought forth the Bible, but Caleb realized he couldn't place his hands on it. They were still shackled behind him.

"Could my hands be freed," Caleb petitioned the judge. "I'd really like to place my hand on that." He nodded toward the black leather book.

The judge nodded his agreement, and the sheriff unlocked the cuffs. Standing tall, Caleb raised his right hand, placed his other on God's Word, and vowed to do what he'd been taught to do his whole life.

"Mr. Jonas," the judge stated after Caleb had been seated. "I'm going to be brief. You've heard all the testimony today. Did you or did you not shoot Bertram Cooley?"

No hesitation. "I did."

"And you claim self-defense?"

"Yes, I do, your honor. He reached for his gun first."

"And where was Miss Bennet in the midst of all this?"

"Cooley had her around the neck. He was using her to shield himself. I think she knew what he was doing. She tried to warn me. Then he shoved her aside."

"So, you're saying Cooley had her as a sort of hostage?"

"Yes, sir."

Mutterings rose for a moment then died away again.

"May I ask, Mr. Jonas, what you were doing out there that night?"

Caleb swallowed. He guessed he should have known this would be coming. "I. . ." *Don't falter, you idiot.* "I'd seen Lyd—Miss Bennet walking down the street. I was concerned about her safety, walking alone at night. So I went to follow her." Truth it may have been, but lame it sounded, even to his ears.

The judge took a painstakingly long time to jot down some

more notes on his raft of papers.

"Are you declaring your innocence, Mr. Jonas?"

"I shot Bertram Cooley in self-defense. I am innocent of inflicting any injury on Miss Bennet. I would never hurt her intentionally." His voice cracked on the last words and he frowned as deeply buried tears threatened to sting his eyes.

"Thank you, Mr. Jonas. We will take a one-hour break for dinner. When we return, I will announce my decision." The gavel banged against the desk, and the flurry of people swarmed toward the exit. Caleb sat in a daze.

Jim Foy approached. "Jonas, how are you doing?"

He merely shrugged.

"Did you get a chance to read those verses?"

Caleb met the doctor's eye. "Yeah. Thanks. They helped. More than you know."

A sad smile spread across Foy's face. "I'm glad." He placed a hand on Caleb's shoulder. "Hungry?"

Caleb shook his head. "If you don't mind, I think I'll just sit here for a while."

"You sure?"

"Yeah, thanks though." He returned a weak smile.

With a gentle clap on the back, his friend was gone, leaving Caleb alone with his thoughts. Sheriff Watkins hung near the back door, seeming to sense Caleb's need to be alone.

All he could do was go over and over the questions asked of him by the judge. It all came down to one thing. . .the one thing that very few of these people understood. He'd never have done this to Lydia, never in a million years. He'd sooner have given his own life than have her lose hers.

He shut his eyes against the distractions of the room and prayed. *Take care of her, God. Heal her. Don't let her die.*

He slowly opened his eyes and stared out the window facing the main street. It held a view of Doc Foy's residence and surgery. "I love her."

nineteen

Sheriff Watkins finally left the little schoolhouse. Caleb was thankful for the time alone, and he made the most of it by alternately praying and meditating on his life.

But the hour was gone too quickly. When the first of the spectators started to return, he looked up from his chair. It was a curious, unsettling feeling as he noted face after face that would not even look at him.

It didn't take long for the throng to assemble. The judge was nearly the last to arrive. The large crowd remained ominously quiet as they watched him shuffle through his papers.

Caleb thought he might die from waiting for the judgment. But at last the low voice came forth.

"I've gone over my notes extensively, rereading all the testimony given. I'm prepared to issue a verdict and a sentence at this time."

Caleb swallowed hard. If his decision was that swift, it was not a good sign.

The somber face regarded the onlookers. "Based on the evidence and Mr. Jonas's own admission, I find him guilty of the shooting of Bertram Cooley."

Caleb's heart jolted to a stop, then slammed painfully against his ribs as the voices began to murmur around the room. He closed his eyes in defeat. There was half of it.

"I had to give serious consideration to the evidence that Mr. Cooley's gun had not been drawn from its holster," the official explained. He glanced back down at his sheet. "Now as to the matter of the attempted murder of Lydia Bennet, frankly I see no evidence that there was indeed any deliberate attempt on her life. Her wounds, other than the knife wound, seemed to have been sustained in a fall. That evidence is sketchy, at best. It was indeed Mr. Cooley's knife, but it is not known who held it."

Caleb felt a small breath of relief issue from his lungs. At least someone believed he hadn't done any harm to Lydia.

The judge's glance swept over the gathering as he went on. "But there was obviously some form of competition over Miss Bennet. Considering the testimony given, I strongly believe that such intense feelings can lead to crimes of passion. Therefore, I am rejecting the plea of self-defense."

The crowd erupted into a fervor. The judge banged his gavel several times, trying to restore order. Caleb felt his insides wrench as he stared blankly at the floor.

"Of the attempted murder of Miss Lydia Bennet, I find Caleb Jonas innocent," the judge declared. "Of the murder of Bertram Cooley, I find him guilty." He hesitated briefly, as if waiting to see whether the crowd would disrupt again. When it did not, he continued. "Based on the assumption that Mr. Cooley was involved in some sort of exchange with Mr. Jonas, I have opted not to sentence him to death."

Caleb was hard pressed to hear the judge over the pounding in his ears, but he strained to listen.

"My sentence is as follows. On the morrow, Caleb Jonas will leave this town."

Caleb felt his spirit deflate as he slowly raised his head and met the stare of the judge.

"Due to the serious nature of the charges leveled against you, Mr. Jonas, I'm afraid this incident will follow you, especially considering your past as a ranger. It would be difficult to imagine any law-abiding town accepting you into its population."

He returned to consult his papers and lifted his eyes to the gathering once more. "As far as the Boxed CJ ranch, it will be auctioned off part by part next week. So ends this trial."

With a bang of his gavel, the judge officially dismissed the throng and ended the proceedings. And Caleb Jonas's life.

❧

Caleb moved about the stables, almost in a trance, collecting the gear he thought he'd need. *Need. For what? Well, for the solitude I always craved,* he thought ironically. *Now I'll have it, that's for sure.*

For his mount he picked the roan-colored horse. . .the one he'd watched Lydia talk to that night. Lydia. He gave himself a mental shake as he braced his arms against the stable wall. That was one name he was going to have to try his hardest to forget.

Caleb was suddenly aware of a shuffle behind him. He turned his head to find the whole crew of hired hands including Willy standing there. Several were twisting their hats in their hands nervously, while others met his eye hesitantly.

"Hey, fellas." He turned to greet them.

"Jonas." It was apparent that Willy had been chosen to be the voice of the group. "We just wanted to say that all of us feel just. . .terrible about all of this. We know you didn't do nothin' wrong."

Caleb looked compassionately at the motley crew, and his heart swelled with gratitude. Here were some true friends. "Thanks, men," he managed in a raspy voice.

Willy stepped forward and handed several saddlebags toward Caleb. "We've kind of taken up a collection, of sorts. Some food stuffs, extry socks and clothes, a few books. . ."

One of the cowboys tried to lighten the mood. "I even threw in my harmonica, Boss."

Caleb smiled. "Not your new one I hope, Jake."

"Yep. Couldn't get the hang of the fool thing anyway."

Caleb could only nod his appreciation. No words would come. Biting his lip, he sauntered over to his horse's stall and led him out, carefully tying the saddlebags near the others.

He mounted swiftly, fearing that each extra moment spent lingering would make the parting that much more painful.

He looked down at his faithful employees. "I know you boys will care for this place the same as you do now." He tried to offer a smile, but only one corner of his mouth would cooperate. Readjusting his Stetson, he pulled back on the reins, preparing to turn the gelding around.

A frantic voice rushed into the midst of the throng.

Caleb swivelled in his saddle to see little Jimmy Tucker pushing his way to the front. The youngster who so often had been his tail.

The boy's dusty face was streaked with tears. Caleb didn't have to guess why he hadn't been present before now. A tender tug wrenched on Caleb's heart. He tried to smile for the boy's sake. "You keep these men in line, Jim."

A sniff or two preceded the boy's quiet answer. "Yes, sir. I will." With that, he raised a hand to his forehead in a salute. It was the first time since Caleb had left the rangers that he'd been shown that courtesy.

Lifting his own salute in return, he quickly wheeled his horse around and left the stable at a swift canter.

❧

It is hard to express the utter isolation of the Wyoming mountains in winter. When the only contact one has with another human being is when looking in a broken piece of mirrored glass every morning to shave.

Caleb had quickly ascended Laramie Peak and gone on. No use tempting fate by being any closer to that town. . .her town.

Through the late summer and early fall, he'd worked almost in a frenzy to erect his modest one-room log cabin. He worked in part because the snows could come early up that high, but also, the intense labor gave him a needed outlet, a place to redirect his thoughts.

But he couldn't deny that on several occasions when he'd been driving a wooden spike into a log he'd wished that Bradley Smyth's head had been on the other end. But from a place inside that was growing larger everyday, he'd immediately rebuke himself and remind himself of the wretched things he used to do. In spite of all he had done or that Bradley Smyth had done, Caleb knew that Jesus had died for both of them. It was a humbling thought.

Other thoughts were almost impossible to deal with. When the bitter north wind howled incessantly around the snug structure and he sat before the blazing fire, all he could picture was Lydia, lovingly bent over a simmering kettle, her blazing hair made even more alive in the fire's light. Or, Lydia sitting companionly beside him while she stitched on a Log Cabin quilt. Those times were the hardest to bear. All he could do was pray that if she were even alive, she would find happiness.

The makeshift calendar he'd tacked to the wall gradually shed pages as the fierceness of winter melted away into the promise of spring. One day, when the sun shone but the temperature hovered barely above freezing, Caleb strapped on his snowshoes and went in search of something for supper.

He'd found sufficient wildlife in the area to at least supply him with food. And he carefully hoarded the few jars of vegetables that Willy had sent. Those were for special occasions. He remembered deeming Christmas as occasion to warrant opening a jar of green beans. But as for the rest of that day, it passed in familiar nothingness. Although he did make an effort to reread the Christmas story from his now well-worn Bible. And he thanked God for the blessing of merely being alive.

As he tromped through the waning snow, he listened intently to the sounds of the few birds that stayed to make the mountains their winter home. The sun was shining brilliantly off the snow-tipped trees, and the air held just a hint of warmth. He stopped to fill his lungs with its freshness.

His gaze fell upon another set of snowshoe prints.

Instinct took over immediately. His head snapped up to quickly scan the area around him. All seemed in order.

Carefully approaching the tracks, he knelt and lightly touched them with his fingers. They were not old. A day or two at the most. Curious. He'd never seen any sign of man around here before. A bit wary, he opted to head back home. He didn't want to attract any undue attention until he discovered who was out here. Placing his shoes back on the path of his tracks, he headed for his cabin.

The rest of the day passed by in monotony. He delved into a jar of carrots and mixed up a batch of biscuits with the bear tallow he'd rendered from one of his bear hunting expeditions.

The night was a calm one, the full moon glistening down on the crystal-flecked snow. Caleb sat before the fire, cleaning his rifle and listening to the snap and hiss of burning wood.

A knock on the door nearly made him lose his grip on the weapon. He stared in complete shock at the barricaded entrance. How long had it been since he'd heard that sound? Then the snowshoe tracks ran through his memory.

Easing up from his stool, he laid aside the rifle and grabbed his Colt from the nearby table. He walked to the door and, standing slightly behind it, lifted up the heavy plank. As he opened it a crack, still keeping a goodly amount of weight against it, he addressed whoever was outside. "Whoever you are, state your business. You best be warned I've got a loaded .45 leveled right at head height."

A mirthful chuckle answered him. Then a familiar voice said, "Glad to see you haven't lost it, Jonas."

Caleb didn't know whether to believe his ears or not. Still leaving his gun at the ready, he carefully pulled the door back.

"Captain McNelly!" Releasing the hammer on the pistol, Caleb grinned and ushered the man into the cabin with a hearty slap on the back. "Man, never thought I'd see you again!"

The older gentlemen laughed with Caleb, his dark eyes twinkling mischievously. He hadn't changed much.

"What are you doing here? Did they kick you out of the corps?"

"Nope. Just gettin' too old. Decided to retire. Let you youngsters have a go at it."

Caleb smiled back, still standing and shaking his head in amazement.

"Oh, just a minute!" McNelly stepped outside and returned with a string of dressed rabbits. "Just in case I interrupted your hunting today."

Caleb laughed. "Still sneaky as ever, I see. So those were *your* shoe tracks."

He nodded. "Doesn't look like you've changed at all—save the acre of hair on your face."

"Yeah, well." Caleb scratched at his beard. "It keeps the cold out."

They took several more seconds to study one another. "Well, what are you doing way up here?" Caleb finally asked.

"First things first," his former superior chided. "I'm pretty near starved. Let's cook up these critters. Then I'll tell you the whole story."

"Agreed."

Three rabbits, several hours, and a good many cups of coffee later, McNelly and Caleb sat and stared at the warming fire.

"I still can't believe they sent you all the way up here," Caleb admitted.

"Hey, when I'm given a job to do, I do it." He smiled. "But I'll have to admit, I jumped at the chance. Especially when I heard what had happened to you last summer."

Caleb shook his head as if trying to shake off the memory. "In a lot of ways it seems like a hundred years ago."

"Well, it might as well be." The captain set his mug down on the dirt floor. "Don't you see, my friend? It's all over now. The truth came out. That Smyth fellow is gone, run out of town—what they should have done to him in the first place. But what he deserved got placed on you instead."

"How did they find out?

"A couple ways, I guess. There were some legal papers of some sort found regarding the sale of the mercantile in town and such. And a young cowhand who'd been aware of the banker's deals with Kid Cooley finally had nerve enough to come forward."

Caleb stood and paced the small room, trying to take in the surprising turn of events. Was it possible? Could it really be true? Or was he having some bizarre dream? He had been away from people for a long time.

Dream or not, one thought pushed constantly to the front of his mind. He turned slowly and faced his old friend. "Did they say anything about Miss Bennet?"

The older gentleman looked at the fire for a moment. "No. 'Fraid not."

Caleb cast his gaze at the floor.

"But," McNelly interjected, "the telegraph was pretty brief."

Caleb nodded in appreciation. Surely they would have said if she'd. . . He swallowed painfully and tried to erase in a single second all the visions he'd collected over the past eight months. "Okay," he whispered. "I'll go back."

The delight was obvious on his friend's face.

"I won't stay though."

A look of defeat crossed McNelly's features, but he nodded. "I guess I can understand that."

"I'll go back. Just for those folks who believed in me. But after that, there's nothing. I've no ranch, no home. . ." He didn't need to reiterate what he already knew was gone.

God had brought him through this trial, but staying in the town where she'd been. . . No, he wasn't strong enough for that.

"I'll pack up a few things."

twenty

Five and a half days into their journey, McNelly and Caleb reached the outskirts of Darby. Caleb reined in his gelding, flooded by a rush of conflicting emotions at the sight of such familiar surroundings. In some ways it felt like he'd been there just yesterday; in others, a hundred years might have gone by.

The captain silently waited for Caleb's signal to continue. With a nod of his black Stetson, Caleb led the way.

From a distance, the town had looked the same, but once he reached the main street, Caleb noted some changes. The mercantile was open again, an unfamiliar name posted where the Bennets' used to be. He hurriedly shifted his focus—there were too many memories at that place.

But it seemed no matter where his gaze fell, the spot held some fragment of a thought, a conversation, a look. He realized more than ever why he couldn't stay in Darby.

Stepping up his pace, Caleb headed for Dr. Foy's residence. At least there he hoped little had changed. When they reached the hitching post, McNelly remained in his saddle. "I'm gonna go see to a room at the boarding house. I'll meet up with you later."

Caleb nodded as he fastened the reins around the post.

The walk to the house seemed to take an eternity. He tried to concentrate on the superficial things to keep his active mind busy. *They had less snow here than up in the mountains. Feels a bit warmer, too.*

Reaching the large front door, he took a deep breath and rapped several times on the brass knocker. He heard some shuffling noises from inside, and a shadow approached the window. When the door flew open, he stood face to face with the man who'd befriended him through it all. Just in seeing

Doc's kind face, Caleb realized how keenly he had missed the man.

Without hesitation, Jim Foy embraced him and drew him into the house. Neither spoke. There didn't seem to be a need.

After a moment, a familiar feminine voice drifted out to them. "Who is it?"

Caleb's breath caught in his throat as he heard her approaching footsteps. Around the corner emerged a glowing Sophia, complete with a figure that gave every indication that a new member would be joining this household in the not-too-distant future.

She stopped short on seeing Caleb and, with a glad cry, threw herself into his arms. "Oh, Caleb! They found you."

A bit self-consciously, Caleb hugged her back. He finally found his voice. "Yeah, they did. And it looks like congratulations are in order around here. I should have known you'd be married by now. But this. . ." He smiled and shook Jim's hand. "I'm extremely happy for you."

Jim beamed as he hugged Sophia next to him. "Yes, she's a fine woman." Then his clear blue eyes returned to Caleb's face. "I really wished you could have stood up with me, you know."

Caleb nodded. "I'd have been proud to."

The threesome suddenly were at a loss for words. The doctor finally released the silence. "Are you staying?"

Caleb shook his head. "No. There's nothing here anymore." Then looking up quickly, he added, "No offense to you two."

"None taken. Will you go out to the ranch, at least?"

A heavy sigh came from deep within. "I dunno. Part of me wants to, but I'm not sure I could see what I worked so hard to build up in someone else's hands."

Jim wagged his head in understanding. "Yeah, that would be tough. But I think you should go anyway. We'll go with you. I could hitch up the rig—"

"Thanks for the thought," Caleb hastily interrupted. "But I really hadn't planned on—"

"You know, Caleb," the doctor urged. "It might be just

what you need. To give you sense of. . .well, to lay to rest some of your unanswered questions. Maybe help you let go of it—if that's what you want."

Tilting his head, Caleb studied his friend's determined look. He might be right. "Well, maybe for a brief look. But I don't want to get real close or anything."

"Agreed. Sophia, go get your wraps."

She skittered off to comply, and Jim grabbed his overcoat from the peg near the door. "Care to ride with us?"

"Nah, I'll stay on old faithful out there."

They soon were ready to disembark and started down the street just as Captain McNelly approached. "Mind if I tag along?" he asked.

"Sure," Caleb muttered. "Just going to look at a ghost ranch." He smiled grimly.

The ride out was spent in companionable silence. Caleb and the captain led the way as the surrey bounced along behind them. Caleb noted every tree, every clump of brush, every landmark that had etched itself onto his brain. It was strange to be riding on the land as an outsider.

About a quarter mile from the buildings, Caleb stopped.

"You want to keep going?" Doc's voice came from behind.

"I don't know. I don't even know who lives here."

"Looks like we're about to find out." McNelly nodded his head toward the dirt path where two riders were trotting out to meet them.

Caleb shifted uneasily in his saddle. He studied the approaching riders. They were good in the saddle, that was obvious. As they got nearer, he frowned in concentration. The one on the left looked a lot like Hal Tucker. Each hoof fall brought them closer, and Caleb stared in stunned silence as he realized it was indeed Hal—and Jake. Two of his old hands.

Their expressions lit up when they saw their former employer.

"Jonas!

"Man, you're back!"

Caleb nudged the roan forward and shook hands with each

in turn. "You two! I can't believe you're still here. Did you get hired by the new owner or something?"

They exchanged glances.

"Not exactly," Jake answered.

"Come see the rest of the guys," Hal urged. "They're still here, too."

Caleb shrugged and followed the pair back toward the buildings.

Everything they passed seemed to be in excellent repair. Fences were strong and tight, buildings and corrals were well kept. He glanced toward the house and noticed that smoke was curling gently from its chimneys.

They rounded the stables, and immediately he was recognized by a throng of cowboys. Dismounting, he accepted with relish their handshakes and hearty cuffs on the back. As he greeted the crowd, he took a moment to scan the corrals. His eyes searched for the brand the cattle now wore. When one steer finally turned the right way, he got a full view of a box with the connected CJ within its confines. He could only stare. What on earth was going on here?

A bellowing voice caused him to turn and greet the round, beaming face of Willy Albert. Moved with sudden emotion, he gripped the man in an embrace.

"Thought somebody had said the boss got back!" Willy chortled. " 'Bout time. I was beginnin' to wonder if you expected all of us to do the work for ya forever."

That brought a good, hearty laugh from the rest of the men.

Jim Foy stepped forward. "I guess there's a few things you need to be filled in on, Jonas."

Caleb nodded in total confusion.

"You see, there *was* an auction," he explained. "Our friendly banker, Mr. Smyth, was in charge. Quite the crowd that turned out that day, too, eh, boys?"

Several men voiced agreement.

"Anyway, everything pretty much went as it came up for bid."

Caleb waited for Jim to elaborate. When he didn't, he

finally broached the subject. "So, who bought it?"

"Hm, let's see," the doctor looked thoughtful for a moment. "I got most of the horses. Willy, you got what—a couple hundred head of cattle?"

Willy nodded with a grin. "Got 'em fer a good price, too."

That brought another round of laughter.

"Wait a minute," Caleb interrupted, overcome with a need to clarify things. "Are you saying that *all* of you bought some of it?"

"Yep," Willy agreed. "That snake-in-the-grass Smyth came in here hoping to line his pretty pockets. Didn't quite go like he planned. What'd you pay for your section of land, Amos?"

"Two bits," came the answer from the rear of the crowd.

"Got my cattle for a little under fifty cents a piece," another hand offered.

Suddenly it was falling into place. Caleb didn't know whether he was going to bust out laughing or cry from sheer joy.

"And I'll have you know," Jim said, "I had to cough up considerably more cash per item—to the tune of one dollar a horse."

The laughter started again. After it had died down, Jim placed a hand on Caleb's shoulder. "Everything is available for resale, if you want it. Asking price is selling price. Now that you're back."

Swamped by overwhelming gratitude and incredible relief, Caleb was at a loss for words. How could he even hope to repay his debt of friendship? These men had believed in him, stood by him, worked for him, and in a sense, saved his world for him. It was more than he could comprehend.

Just then, Sophia stepped forward. "Jim, I think you should tell him about the house."

"Oh, yes." Jim hesitated a moment. "Someone else bought the house, but they're not interested in selling it back to you. They've made it very clear that they plan to stay."

Caleb frowned. Why would someone want just the house? "Well, maybe if I talked to them," he offered. "I could pay them a fair amount for it."

Jim shook his head. "I don't know. They're awfully adamant about staying."

"Yeah, I know you said that. But if—"

"The house is not for sale."

A new voice cut in from behind him. A voice filled with as much determination as Doc had indicated. But a voice that held an edge of gentleness to it that Caleb had only heard in his dreams for far too long.

Turning around slowly, Caleb stood and drank in the vision before him. Her coppery red curls were trying to escape their combs. Her green eyes stared straight into his soul.

"I'm sorry, Mr. Jonas," she spoke again. He savored just watching her full lips move. "But the house is not for sale. I fully plan on staying right here." Her emerald eyes glinted mischievously as she met his gaze unwaveringly. "However," her voice softened. "I wouldn't be opposed to sharing."

Caleb shook his head in wonder. How often had he assumed she was dead? How many times had his being ached when he realized he would never feel her within his arms? To read with, to laugh with, to work together side by side, to raise a family together, to grow old at each other's side. And now, here she stood.

"Lydia," his voice refused to rise above a whisper. "I—" A break in his throat forced him to stop. Thankfully, Jim took the cue.

"Alright, everybody, let's head up to the house. There's got to be coffee around here somewhere, right, Willy?"

The crowd dispersed, but Caleb was barely aware of it. He did have the presence of mind to lead Lydia to the shelter of the stables, but he never released her hand. He was too afraid to let her go.

Lydia squeezed his hand tightly as she followed his lead. Once in the confines of the stable, Caleb turned toward her. They stared at one another for a timeless moment. She smiled tenderly as he reached over and stroked her cheeks, then carefully traced with his thumb the scar on her forehead.

His raspy voice, magnified with emotion, finally broke the silence. "When I think of what it took to wake me up to the fact of how much I need you. . ."

"Sshhh." She placed a finger on his lips. "This was not your fault, so stop blaming yourself. All that matters is that you're here now."

Caleb studied her intently. "And you really want *me?"*

"No one else," she murmured. *"If I had but one chance, to meet the mountain's son, I think I'd fall in love. . .and join him in his run."*

"No," he corrected her. "I'm done running." Grabbing her shoulders, he drew her tightly to himself.

The walls finally fell. Caleb let tears fall unhindered down his whiskered cheeks. For a long while they stayed that way, simply holding each other, trying to savor the moment after so much pain. It felt good. It felt right.

When Caleb finally eased her from his chest, he looked intently into her eyes. "Lydia Bennet, will you marry me?"

She looked up at him from under her lashes, suddenly feeling playful. "It's a bit late," she scolded him teasingly. "But, yes, Caleb. I want nothing more than to marry you."

His mouth moved to a grin. "I love you."

She smiled back, feeling a lightness she'd never known before. "Not nearly as much as I love you."

"Really?" He raised his eyebrows in the challenge.

"Nope."

"Well, I guess I'll have to spend the rest of my life proving it to you."

"It's a bet!"

Caleb laughed. "Okay, little miss. Let's start right now." He lowered his head, and Lydia's eyes fluttered shut in anticipation. His lips met hers with a sweet, soulful longing known only to those who have lost—and regained. Through it came all the forbidden moments they'd been denied. All the times they'd come so close.

She finally pulled away and buried her head against his shoulder. "Okay," she whispered. "You win."

epilogue

Lydia idly tapped the quill against the paper before her. An intermittent breeze that was playing with the lace panel in the window lifted the edge of the paper. She raised her eyes to study the scene outside. From the bedroom window, she could see Caleb and a few of the hands getting ready to head out and mend fence. A never-ending job, she was beginning to discover.

Caleb caught her eye and tipped his head to one side with a playful smile. Lydia grinned back and waved. He doffed his Stetson and bowed his head with exaggeration. She couldn't restrain her laughter. With one last wave, he swung around on his mount and trotted after the others.

As her chuckles subsided, Lydia thought of her father. Caleb was so much like him. *Daddy. . .* Bittersweet memories flooded over her—and reminded her of the task at hand.

She dipped the nib in the inkwell and sighed as the pen touched the paper.

15 June, 1881
Mrs. John Bennet
18 Washington Street
Boston, Massachusetts

She still found it strange to be writing to her mother rather than simply having tea together. It had been nearly ten months since Mother had left for Boston to live with her sister.

Dear Mother,

Lydia sighed. Best to start with the latest—and most exciting—happenings.

I am writing to inform you of Jim and Sophia's happy news. Sophia delivered a healthy boy on the 10th of June. Both of them are doing splendidly and Jim couldn't be more proud. They've named him John James Foy.

Lydia's eyes misted, but she pressed on.

I think Daddy would be proud, don't you? Sophia is adamant on calling him John, but both Jim and Caleb have let the name "JJ" slip more than a few times.

Her tears turned to a smile, knowing that her father would have dubbed the youngster that himself.

But on to what I initially wanted to write to you about.

This is where it got more difficult. But Lydia knew she had to do this. It was long overdue. During the times she and Caleb had been studying the Bible together, verses had jumped out at her, convicting her and encouraging her. It was time.

I'm sorry you weren't able to be make it for the wedding. It was so lovely, Mother. We had it right here at the ranch house. The wild flowers were aplenty, and the weather cooperated beautifully. The hands even went so far as to tie ribbons on the posts of the corrals, which the steers promptly ate.

Poor Sophia had to sit through the short ceremony due to the fact that little John was due to arrive at any moment. As it was, he kept us waiting a few more days. But aside from all that, I can't begin to explain all that being Caleb's wife means to me. Truly, I've never been happier.

Lydia still wasn't sure where her mother stood on the issue of her marriage to Caleb. After Lydia had awakened from her head injury, her mother had made it very clear she felt it was time to leave Darby. But taking hope from Jim and Sophia's newfound courage, Lydia refused to comply. In spite of the fact that she didn't know where Caleb was, she was convinced she was doing the right thing by staying in Darby. Somehow it would all work out.

I know that we've had our share of misunderstandings, but I want you to know I'm sorry for the grief I caused you over my foolish pride and other shortcomings.

If there was anything that the long winter had taught Lydia, it was to see herself for who she was. When one faces death, she'd thought, and lives, it is foolish to think that one can go on living as before. The bleakness of the desolate season had given her ample time to sort out what aspects of her character were and were not pleasing to the Almighty.

I want nothing more than for you to have the opportunity to come and visit us here on the ranch. And I know Sophia is anxious to show off your new grandson to you.

A smile crept across Lydia's face at the thought of her father's namesake being the one to soften his grandmother's heart.

Please accept my deepest apologies, my sincerest love, and my earnest invitation. Give Aunt Catherine our greetings and hopes that all is well with her family.

There. That was all she could do. She carefully blotted the last several sentences and studied what she'd written. From here, it would be her mother's choice. She raised the pen to sign off.

With affection, your daughter,

The pen began to form an *L* as she was so accustomed to signing her name, but she stopped midstroke and with great pride and a deliberate hand reformed the letter.

Mrs. Caleb Jonas

A Letter To Our Readers

Dear Reader:

In order that we might better contribute to your reading enjoyment, we would appreciate your taking a few minutes to respond to the following questions. When completed, please return to the following:

Rebecca Germany, Managing Editor
Heartsong Presents
PO Box 719
Uhrichsville, Ohio 44683

1. Did you enjoy reading *The Mountain's Son?*
   - ❑ Very much. I would like to see more books by this author!
   - ❑ Moderately
     I would have enjoyed it more if ________________

   ____

2. Are you a member of **Heartsong Presents**? ❑Yes ❑No
   If no, where did you purchase this book? ________________

   ____

3. What influenced your decision to purchase this book? (Check those that apply.)

❑ Cover	❑ Back cover copy
❑ Title	❑ Friends
❑ Publicity	❑ Other________________

4. How would you rate, on a scale from 1 (poor) to 5 (superior), the cover design? ________________

5. On a scale from 1 (poor) to 10 (superior), please rate the following elements.

___Heroine ___Plot

___Hero ___Inspirational theme

___Setting ___Secondary characters

6. What settings would you like to see covered in **Heartsong Presents** books?___________________

____

____

7. What are some inspirational themes you would like to see treated in future books?______________

____

____

8. Would you be interested in reading other **Heartsong Presents** titles? ❑ Yes ❑ No

9. Please check your age range:
❑ Under 18 ❑ 18-24 ❑ 25-34
❑ 35-45 ❑ 46-55 ❑ Over 55

10. How many hours per week do you read? ________

Name_____________________________________
Occupation________________________________
Address___________________________________
City______________State__________Zip__________